THE LITTLE BOOK OF MANCHESTER UNITED

Written by **Ian Welch**

THE LITTLE BOOK OF

MANCHESTER UNITED

This edition first published in the UK in 2007
By Green Umbrella Publishing

www.gupublishing.co.uk

Publishers Jules Gammond and Vanessa Gardner

Printed and bound in Poland

ISBN: 978-1-906635-38-1

Contents

Aston:
John Aston Senior and John Aston Junior

BORN 23 SEPTEMBER 1921, JOHN Aston Senior began his Manchester United career on 18 September 1946 when he made his League debut against Chelsea at inside-forward. Matt Busby switched Aston's position to full-back, not only changing the number on his back, but also bringing out the best of his talent. Aston blossomed as a full-back bringing his expertise in pace and accuracy to a defensive position which he utilised to the full when he faced Stanley Matthews in the 1948 FA Cup Final.

BELOW John Aston, Senior

During the difficult 1950-51 season, the versatile Aston was moved forward on several occasions giving him the opportunity to score 15 goals. He won 17 England caps before injury cut his career short. He then returned to Old Trafford

ABOVE John Aston Jr (r) taps home the opening goal as Chelsea's Peter Bonetti (l) and Joe Kirkup (c) watch helplessly

MIDDLE John Aston in a heading duel with Adolfo of Benfica in the European Cup Final at Wembley, 29 May 1968

as a youth team coach and, in 1970, became chief scout for the club, a position he held for two years. He remained closely associated with the team and watched his son, John Aston Junior, also make his name at Old Trafford.

Born the year after his father's debut on 28 June 1947, John Junior settled well at Old Trafford, turning professional in 1964. Not as glamorous as Best or Law, Aston Junior was often given a hard time by the home crowd who thought he lacked imagination, but he was nippy and direct, and he remained a loyal and committed player. Matt Busby was impressed and recognised his contribution to the team and he was a member of the 1967 Championship-winning side.

It was in the 1968 European Cup Final where Aston really shone. It became the pinnacle of his career as he repeatedly managed to pass Benfica's Adolfo on the left wing. He lost his first-team place after breaking his leg and was transferred to Luton Town for £30,000 in 1972.

Atkinson

RON ATKINSON'S FIRST LEAGUE job was as manager of Cambridge United in 1974. He had already gained experience with non-League clubs Witney Town and Kettering Town and went on to succeed Dave Sexton at Old Trafford in June 1981 after proving his worth with First Division West Bromwich Albion for three consecutive seasons.

Although United never finished lower than fourth in the League while he was at the helm, the Championship went to his home town, Liverpool, five seasons in a row. However, he won the FA Cup twice, claiming victory over Brighton in 1983 and Everton in 1985 with United setting a club record of ten consecutive League victories at the start of the 1985-86 season.

Renowned for spending large amounts on players, Atkinson only once paid more than £1 million for a player and that was for Bryan Robson who would be a loyal servant. The following season poor form cost Atkinson his job at Old Trafford and he returned to West Brom before moving to Atletico Madrid. He also managed Sheffield Wednesday twice as well as Aston Villa and Coventry City. His successor at Old Trafford was a certain Alex Ferguson, who joined the club on 6 November 1986.

RIGHT Ron Atkinson attends a press conference

FAR RIGHT A thoughtful Ron Atkinson watches a match from the dugout

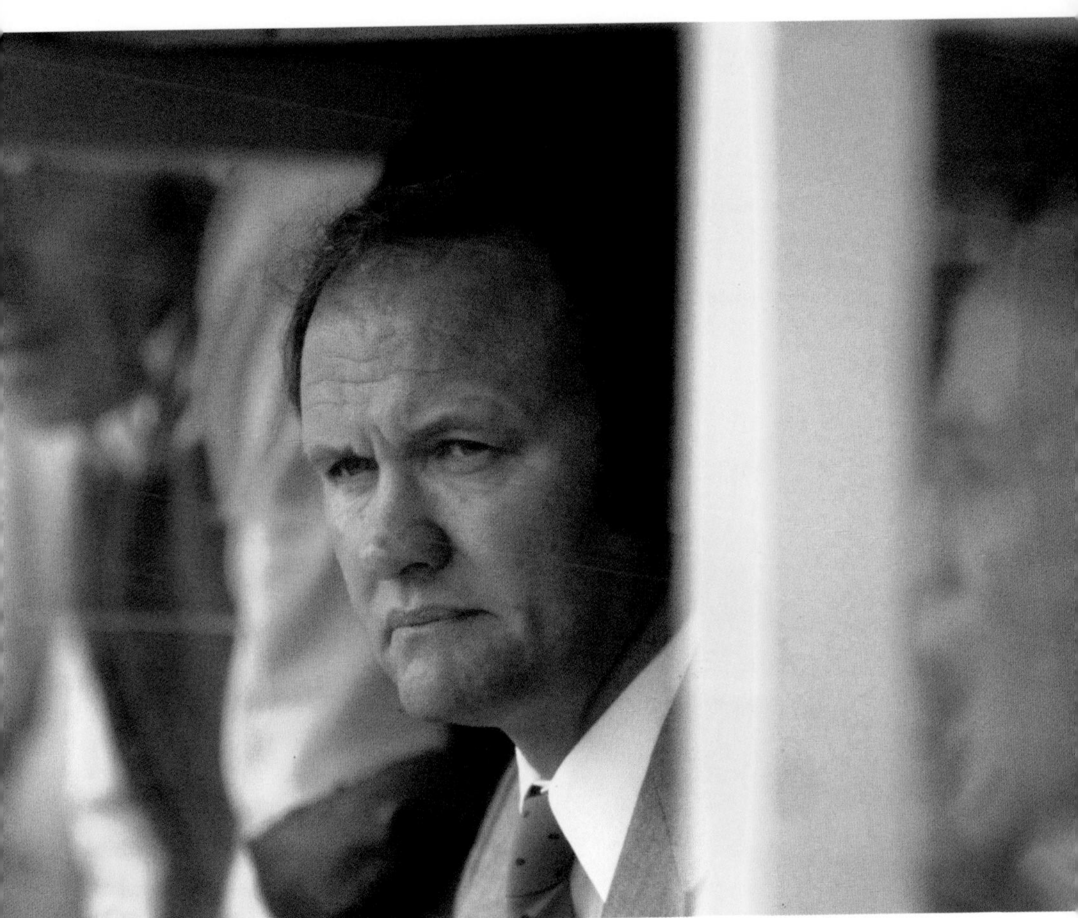

RIGHT Beckham celebrates to the crowd after scoring a goal during the Premiership match against Everton, August 1997

BELOW Old Trafford in 2007

Attendances

THE 76,962 SUPPORTERS WHO crowded into Old Trafford on 25 March 1939 were not Manchester United fans. They had come to watch the FA Cup semi-final between Grimsby Town and Wolves. For many years, the record attendance for a Manchester United home game came on 27 December 1920 when 70,504 watched their team lose 3-1 to an Aston Villa side they had beaten 4-3 in the counterpart fixture just two days earlier.

This, however, has been beaten on numerous occasions following a new boost in Old Trafford's seating capacity that was unveiled in 2006.

On 31 March 2007, 76,098 saw United go in at half time trailing Blackburn Rovers by 1-0 but second-half strikes from Scholes, Carrick, Park and Solskjaer helped redress the balance. Attendances over recent seasons have been 75,304 (2008-09), 75,691 (2007-08), 75,826 (2006-07) and 68,765 (2005-06).

The ground's record attendance for a World Cup match saw 37,000 cheer on Hungary and Portugal in a Group 3 match in 1966. Old Trafford has also hosted the 2003 UEFA Champions League Final, with 63,215 watching an all-Italian clash as AC Milan emerged victorious after a penalty shoot-out with arch-rivals Juventus.

Beckham

DAVID BECKHAM WAS BORN ON 2 May 1975 and signed professionally for United in 1992 after joining as a trainee in 1991. He had come to United's attention after winning a Bobby Charlton skills competition at the age of 11. He made his first-team debut in September 1992 – coming on as a substitute at Brighton – but he had to wait a further two years for another chance and he made the most of it by scoring against Galatasaray in the European Cup.

He gained a regular place in midfield during 1995-96, scoring eight goals during 32 appearances and collecting an FA Cup winner's medal. The opening game against Wimbledon the following season was to mark the start of the David Beckham phenomenon when he scored from 57 yards in the dying minutes of the game.

Beckham made the transition from promising youngster to England's main creative force in just one season, making his debut under Glen Hoddle in September 1996 in Moldova. He enjoyed a momentous season and collected a second Championship medal and was voted the PFA's Young Player of the Year. Despite immense interest in his relationship with Victoria Adams (Posh Spice), Beckham continued to impress on the field, becoming United's top scorer during the 1997-98 season. But the World Cup in 1998 saw Beckham sent off after retaliation against an Argentinian player in a second-round match and many blamed him for England losing the game.

ABOVE Beckham scores the opening goal during the league match between Villa and United at Villa Park, 2003

He returned from the World Cup to vitriolic abuse, but quickly knuckled down and proved wrong all those who thought his career in English football was over. He went on to captain the England side four years later and, despite going out in the quarter-finals to Brazil, the team returned home as heroes. Beckham enjoyed further success at Old Trafford including the 1998-99 Treble before his departure to Real Madrid in June 2003.

After winning La Liga championship in his final season with the club he joined LA Galaxy in 2007 and also enjoyed a loan spell with AC Milan in 2009. His move to Milan has helped prolong his England career and he has now amassed 112 caps, more than any outfield player in the history of English football.

Berbatov

DIMITAR BERBATOV IS A CLASSY centre-forward, pairing the ability to ruthlessly find the net inside the box with magical touches outside of it.

Berbatov started out at Bulgarian side CSKA Sofia where his talent quickly attracted the attention of Bundesliga club Bayer Leverkusen who made their move for the front man in January 2001. Although he was national team captain and Bulgarian Player of the Year in 2002, 2004, 2005 and 2007, he made a slow start to his time in Germany albeit regularly shining in the Champions League.

He was eventually lured to the Premier League when Tottenham signed him in July 2006 for a reported £10.9 million fee. He was an instant hit at White Hart Lane scoring his first competitive goal two minutes into his home League debut against Sheffield United. He went on to score 23 goals in his opening season, which he matched again in 2007-08.

After months of speculation linking him with a move to Old Trafford in the summer of 2008, Sir Alex Ferguson finally got his man on transfer deadline day with just minutes to go. Berbatov signed a four-year contract on 1 September 2008 for an undisclosed fee, with Fraizer Campbell heading to White Hart Lane on a season-long loan as part of the deal.

Berbatov opened his account for the Reds in the same month with two goals away at Aalborg in the Champions League and finished his first season with 14 goals in 42 appearances. Many still feel though that the best is yet to come.

BELOW Fabricio Coloccini of Newcastle United is unable to stop Dimitar Berbatov scoring

Best

ON 16 AUGUST 1961, GEORGE BEST signed as an apprentice for United and went on to become one of the most prolific professionals of all time. The 'Belfast Boy', born on 22 May 1946, went on to sign professionally in May 1963, making his League debut against West Bromwich Albion in September, but remained in the reserves until December that year when he scored in a 5-1 victory. He kept his place on the team and went on to play 466 League, Cup and European games, scoring 178 goals.

Although Best won 37 caps for Northern Ireland – he made his debut in April 1964 – he never actually played in the finals of a major tournament. Not only did he make a name for himself with his goalscoring, Best was renowned for taking on his opponents which was exciting for his fans. Women, particularly, took a shine to Best and football's popularity during the 1960s blossomed alongside his cult status. Best was also gifted at making space for his teammates, notably Bobby Charlton and Denis Law.

Nicknamed 'El Beatle' by the Portuguese after a European Cup match against Benfica in 1966, Best had become football's answer to the Liverpudlian pop idols with his entertaining football and rebel lifestyle. United won the Championship in 1967 and during the following season he enjoyed his greatest success, scoring 28 League goals and inspiring the team to become the first English club to win the European Cup. 1968 saw Best given the titles of Player of the Year, in both England and Northern Ireland, and European Footballer of the Year.

BELOW George Best against Fulham, 1971

ABOVE George in action during the Division One match against Everton played at Old Trafford, in 1968

Two seasons later, however, Best was involved in a number of clashes with referees, United started to go downhill, and late nights fuelled with alcohol added to the slippery slope. Matt Busby's retirement in 1969 seemed to mark the end for George Best. He was fined £100 and received a month's suspension for knocking the ball from the hands of a referee during a League Cup semi-final against Manchester City,

During the 1968-69 season, his performance both on and off the pitch was becoming erratic, but he always remained a difficult opponent. At the end of the 1970 season he was sent off while playing for Northern Ireland for spitting and throwing mud at the referee.

Despite being the top United scorer in May 1971 with 18 goals, his relationship with the management team at United was suffering. In 1972, after failing to turn up to training, manager Frank O'Farrell dropped him, fined him two weeks' wages, gave him extra training and ordered him to return to digs. He then failed to report for Northern Ireland and in May 1972 he announced his retirement while in Spain. He did return but only scored four goals in 1972-73.

George Best played his last game for United on 1 January 1974 aged 27. He went on to play for a variety of clubs in England, Scotland and America but never again reached his outstanding form. He died in November 2005, aged 59, losing his battle with illnesses linked to alcoholism, and his death was mourned worldwide.

Brown

RIGHT Wes Brown celebrates after scoring the opening goal against Liverpool, March 2008

WES BROWN, BORN 13 OCTOBER 1979, signed for United in November 1996 and despite injury setbacks, including a broken ankle, was set to become the team's strongest defender for many years. In his first full season his performances for the reserves and juniors – winning a Lancashire FA Youth Cup winner's medal and a Lancashire League Division One medal as well as the Denzil Haroun Young Player of the Year award – earned Brown his place on the first team, making his debut against Leeds in May 1998.

He is a solid, reliable defender who cemented his regular place when deputising for the injured Denis Irwin at full-back. His established international career at Under-18 and Under-21 levels ensured Brown a step up to the England team during the 1998-99 season, when he received his first cap under Kevin Keegan playing against Hungary in Budapest. Knee ligament injuries during 1999-2000 and his broken ankle at the end of the 2002-03 season were devastating for Brown, but he returned to full fitness and regained his place in the first team and earned himself an England recall.

Following the arrival of Vidic who struck up an understanding with Ferdinand, Brown found opportunities limited but with Gary Neville out injured for 2007-08, the versatile defender slotted in naturally at right-back and has signed a contract that keeps him with the club until 2012.

Bruce

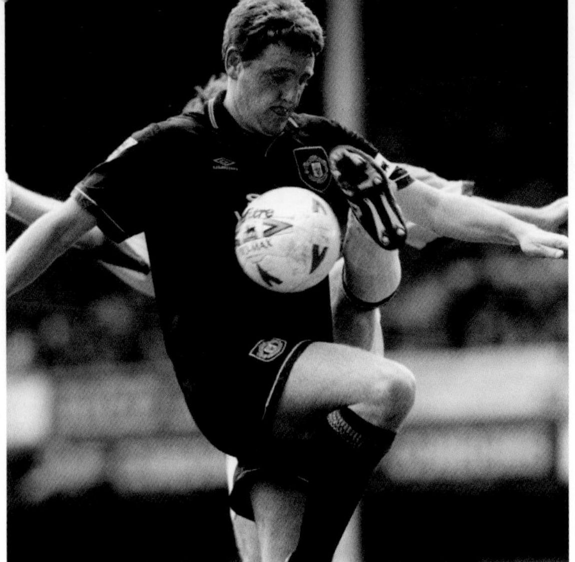

ABOVE Bruce in action during a Premiership match against West Ham United at Upton Park, May 1995

STEVE BRUCE IS ONE OF ONLY 33 players to have appeared in more than 300 League games for United – he played a total of 410 times for the club. Bruce was born 31 December 1960 and began his career with Gillingham, having signed professionally for them in October 1978. The general consensus was that although he was committed, he lacked genuine talent – this turned out not to be true, as his illustrious career shows.

He was renowned for his determination and leadership which became an essential part of the most successful era in United's history. Bruce signed for United in December 1987 after a successful career at Norwich City who he joined in July 1984 on his departure from Priestfield. His grit and determination turned out to be just the qualities that United were looking for and he became their most reliable defender.

He had a seven-year partnership with Gary Pallister, whose pace and ball control complemented his own organisational skills. For a while, he was the club's penalty taker, which helped increase his scoring rate and in his eight and a half seasons he scored 51 times. He also scored the highest ever total for a defender during a single season in 1990-91 with 19 goals.

In 1992, Bruce took over the captaincy from Bryan Robson and in his four years as captain he lifted three Premiership trophies, the FA Cup and the League Cup, including the Double in 1993-94 and 1995-96. Bruce never got a full England call-up and left for Birmingham City (who he later managed) on a free transfer in 1996. He has also managed Sheffield United, Huddersfield, Crystal Palace and Wigan and is now the new boss at Sunderland.

Buchan

RIGHT Buchan during a Division One match against Leicester City at Old Trafford, September 1980

ANOTHER DEFENDER THAT MADE an impression at United, although earlier than Steve Bruce, was Martin Buchan, born 6 March 1949. After a successful career at Aberdeen, where he had been made captain aged 20, he led the team to a Scottish Cup victory. In 1971, he made his debut for Scotland – he went on to win 34 caps – and was voted Scottish Player of the Year.

Aberdeen decided to sell their young captain and Buchan chose United over the more successful Liverpool and Leeds clubs of the time. Frank O'Farrell paid £135,000 for Buchan who wasted no time in justifying the fee. Six months later, Tommy Docherty took over as manager, but despite relegation in 1974, once Buchan took over as captain of the team, United bounced back by winning the Second Division Championship in 1975. Then, in 1976, United reached the FA Cup Final but were bitterly disappointed when Southampton won by a single goal.

The following year saw United back in the Final with Liverpool. Despite the opposing side boasting Kevin Keegan, United won a memorable 2-1 victory.

Buchan was the first post-war player to captain both a Scottish and an English Cup-winning side. Persistent injuries led him to hang up his boots in 1983, and he went on to work for a sportswear company promoting football boots.

Busby

ABOVE Sir Matt Busby, 1991

THE STADIUM AT OLD TRAFFORD was a bombed-out wreck when Matt Busby arrived in October 1945. Initially offered a three-year contract by Chairman James Gibson, Busby argued for a term of five years. He wanted to realise his vision which he knew would take time and patience. He also demanded to be given the authority to appoint his own staff and act on his own judgement, asking for both power and responsibility.

The first thing Busby did was to put Jimmy Murphy in charge of the reserve team and heavily involve him with the youth project. Their working partnership was to last for almost 30 years. One by one, the United players returned from the war, most of whom had not seen more than one season of first-team action. All were keen to learn from Busby, who set about preparing his team with a number of positional changes, the results of which were to prove invaluable.

Johnny Carey found his niche at full-back, while John Aston Senior discovered his forte as a defender. Henry Cockburn became a half-wing and Jimmy Delaney transferred from Celtic to form the 'famous five' in the forwards alongside Pearson, Rowley, Mitten and Morris. United ended the 1946-47 season as runners-up in the League. In 1948 they won the FA Cup, beating Blackpool 4-2 to become the first of three great teams.

Busby, who was knighted in 1968 and given the freedom of the City of Manchester, died in 1994. His statue stands outside Old Trafford in Sir Matt Busby Way.

Busby Babes

MATT BUSBY ASSUMED MANAGE-rial control of United mid-season in October 1945. His vision was to use the youth development programme to produce the club's own players and it was in November 1951, after journalist Tom Jackson of the *Manchester Evening News* watched Jackie Blanchflower and Roger Byrne, aged 18 and 21, make their debut against Liverpool at Anfield, that he nicknamed them the 'United Babes'. Not long after, Busby was joined to the name and the 'Busby Babes' were born.

RIGHT Duncan Edwards throwing in the ball, 1957

BELOW Matt Busby with his 'Babes' (l-r) Albert Scanlon, Colin Webster, John Doherty, Tony Hawesworth, Alec Dawson and Paddy Kennedy

The Busby Babes roll-call included Johnny Berry, Jackie Blanchflower, Roger Byrne, Bobby Charlton, Eddie Colman, Duncan Edwards, Mark Jones, Wilf McGuinness, David Pegg, Albert Scanlon, Tommy Taylor, Dennis Viollet, Liam Whelan and Ray Wood. Although not all the Babes had grown up through the youth programme, they were part of the phenomenon that hit English football during the 1950s.

The reign of the Busby Babes was only brought to an end by the Munich air disaster in which eight members of the team were killed. Busby strove to create a youth scheme that included four or five teams on each tier of the programme. The foundations were already in place with the Manchester United Junior Athletic Club having been formed in 1938 by the then secretary Walter Crickmer and chairman James Gibson.

The MUJAC, which had encouraged the likes of John Aston Senior, set the model that Busby was to develop and it was with the experience of chief scouts Louis Rocca and his successor Joe Armstrong that helped the programme achieve success. The aim was to seek out talented young players and enhance their abilities by giving them the chance to train with professional trainers and coaches.

Armstrong was particularly adept at persuading anxious parents that their talented young sons would do well at United. It was his foresight to see the potential in schoolboy players, such as Charlton and Edwards, that gave the club the young talent it needed. Attendances began to grow at youth games as word about the success and talent of the team spread and, in 1953, Matt Busby took his young team to Zurich to compete in the International Youth Cup. Despite the youth of the team they were incredibly mature players and Matt Busby is said to have disliked the nickname.

The Babes were primed to take over the first team but the transition was gradual and it was not until the mid-1950s that all elements Busby thought were necessary were in place. The team beat the League Champions Chelsea in November 1955 and it was from then on that the team made its ascent, going on to win the League Cup in 1957, the FA Cup in 1956 and 1957 and the Charity Shield. The last time the Busby Babes lined up together on the pitch was 5 February 1958 in Belgrade.

Byrne

ROGER BYRNE, BORN 8 FEBRUARY 1929, was possibly one of Matt Busby's most astute signings for United. Part of the youth programme, Byrne played at wing-half, inside-forward and then wing again in both the 'A' team and the Reserves, but on his first-team debut in November 1951 he played at left-back. He made 24 appearances in his first season, making a reputation for himself during the latter half going back to his familiar role as left-wing, scoring seven times and helping United to their first Championship in 41 seasons.

In October 1952 Byrne asked for a transfer, unhappy with his place on the wing. Busby immediately reinstated him to the position of left-back and he played for the remainder of the season in his favoured position. When Johnny Carey decided to retire in May 1953 aged 34, Allenby Chilton stood in as captain, but the real potential lay with Byrne, who assumed the role in February 1954. Busby had decided by this time it was necessary to bring more young blood into the side and Byrne became mentor to the young Busby Babes.

Despite his tendency to tell his manager when he did not like something, Busby and Byrne held each other in high regard and Busby liked his captain's leadership qualities. In 1954 he was picked to play for England against Scotland and it turned out to be the first of 33 consecutive caps for his country, despite never scoring and even missing two penalties against Brazil and Yugoslavia. Roger Byrne won three Championship winner's medals with United before his death in Munich.

BELOW Roger Byrne clears the ball

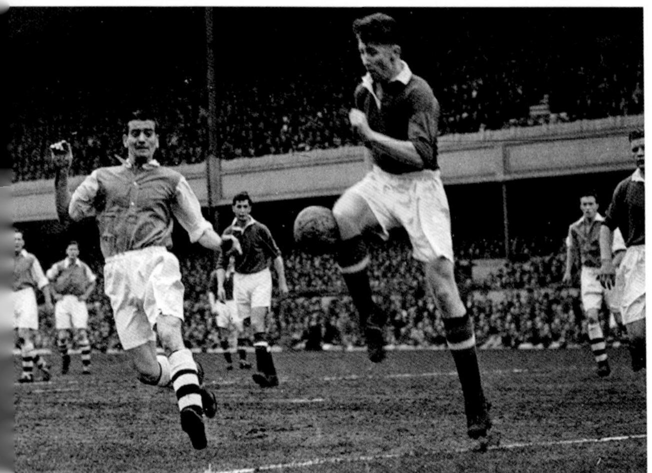

Cantona

ALEX FERGUSON DESCRIBED ERIC Cantona as "...the catalyst for the Championships. He brought a vision that we did not have before. Although I thought we were getting there, Cantona certainly accelerated it. He was an absolutely phenomenal player."

In just over four years at United, Cantona was an essential part of the club winning the League Championship four times. This was exceptional considering that the club had not won it for 26 years. Cantona, like George Best, was worshipped by the fans who called him 'the King', or 'God'. Cantona, however, remained a man of mystery. He had a love of poetry, art and philosophy that didn't somehow fit with the perception of a Premiership footballer. He was also an unconventional striker who preferred to drop off deep and play just behind the forward line. He had the rare talent of being able to create space and time for himself.

Cantona was born in Paris on 24 May 1966 and after spells at various clubs in France signed for Leeds in February

ABOVE Cantona shields the ball from Brian Gayle of Sheffield United during a Premiership match at Old Trafford in 1993

CANTONA

RIGHT Cantona in action during the FA Premiership match between Manchester United and Middlesbrough at Old Trafford, October 1995

1992, joining United in November that year for £1 million. He quickly settled into his new team and signs of his influence were seen with a 4-1 victory over Tottenham in January 1993 – United only lost one of 23 games in which he played during 1992-93. Six months after signing Cantona, the club were Champions. In his first full season, United won their first ever Double and he became the first foreigner to ever be voted PFA Player of the Year.

A few years later, however, trouble loomed and, after attacking a Crystal Palace fan who was verbally abusing him in January 1995, Cantona was sentenced to two weeks' imprisonment. This was reduced on appeal to 120 hours' community service, but without Cantona (banned for eight months), United failed in their defence of the Double and finished as runners-up in both the League and the FA Cup.

In October 1995, Cantona returned and managed to keep his temper under control. He was determined that United would reclaim both titles. The closest challenger at the time was Newcastle, but they were no contest for United with Cantona on the pitch. The double Double was won in 1996 and he redeemed himself.

The following season Cantona captained the side to a fourth Premiership title. However, he took United's failure to reach the European Cup Final particularly badly and he decided to retire from football a week after lifting the Premiership trophy. Of the 19 penalties that he took for United, Cantona only missed two. He scored 80 League and Cup goals, 14 with his head.

Carey

JOHN JOSEPH CAREY, BORN 23 February 1919, used his brains as well as his brawn during his spell at United using a style which completely changed the way full-backs play. On a visit to Dublin, long-time chief scout, Louis Rocca, was impressed by his thoughtful way on the pitch and Rocca signed the young Irishman for £250. He described him later as the best, cheapest and most successful signing he ever made. Carey went on to captain one of England's greatest teams as well as setting a record by playing for both the Republic of Ireland and Northern Ireland.

In his time at United, Carey played 344 times and scored 18 goals from his position as full-back. He made his debut for the club in September 1937 at the age of 18, playing inside-forward, and helped the club to be promoted from the Second Division. It was also during this year that he won his first international cap for the Republic of Ireland. Joining the British Army in 1939, he served in North Africa and Italy. During this time he was fortunate to play football and made guest appearances for several Italian clubs.

On his return from World War II, Matt Busby had been newly installed as United's manager. Carey's position as inside-forward was taken by Pearson and Busby's decision to play him as full-back was pure luck. The United board were not impressed by the decision as Carey did not fit the description of a big, brawny lad who could tackle hard and Busby nearly lost his job. Busby's determination to stick to his guns, however, brought great rewards for the club. Carey became captain and found his niche enabling him to organise the defence and attack from deep down the pitch. Success in the League, however, eluded the team.

This changed in 1948 when the team won the FA Cup against Blackpool. A year later Carey captained the Republic of Ireland team when they became the first foreign team to beat England on their own soil. He retired in 1953 and went on to coach and manage Blackburn Rovers.

ABOVE John Carey, one of United's celebrated Irishmen, was a star of the early postwar era

Carrick

RIGHT Michael Carrick with his new United shirt

BELOW A happy Michael Carrick after scoring his first goal of the 2008-09 season

MICHAEL CARRICK HAD HIS detractors at the start of his United career – with some grumblings about his £18 million transfer fee – but a succession of sterling performances has silenced the doubters.

Even after his debut in the 2006-07 season, in which he carved out a formidable partnership with Paul Scholes as the Reds reclaimed the title, some people predicted he'd slip down the pecking order after the arrival of Owen Hargreaves. But Carrick has become ever more important to United, maturing into one of English football's most sophisticated and classy passing midfielders.

The first of Carrick's three League titles with United to date was also the first major honour of his professional career having played for West Ham and Spurs while they were going through barren spells.

When he first joined United he was encouraged by Sir Alex Ferguson to push forward and eventually weighed in with six strikes from midfield in 2006-07. Indeed his second goal, at home to Reading in the FA Cup, was shortlisted for the club's Goal of the Season award (won by Scholes away to Villa).

Carrick may have only scored three goals in 2007-08 but his all-round contribution to the cause could not be questioned as the Reds were crowned Champions of England and Europe. No wonder then that club and player agreed a new four-year deal in May 2008 to keep him at United until June 2012.

He immediately started to repay that faith in the 2008-09 season with the club retaining the Premiership, winning the Carling Cup and reaching the Champions League Final. He has scored a dozen goals in nearly 150 games and has also cemented his place in the England midfield.

Champions League

HAVING BEEN THE FIRST ENGLISH club to win the European Cup in 1968, by the time United next won the League title 25 years later the competition had been expanded and renamed the Champions League. United's return to Europe's flagship competition in 1993-94 saw them ease past Honved before going out on the away goal rule to Galatasaray. The following year saw the introduction of the group stage and, despite gaining revenge on Galatasaray with a 4-0 home victory, United failed to progress to the second round after suffering defeats at Barcelona and IFK Gothenburg.

Despite losing three of the six group matches in 1996-97, United managed to

BELOW Ole Gunnar Solskjaer celebrates scoring the second goal during the Champions League Final against Bayern Munich in the Nou Camp, 1999

ABOVE Manchester United celebrate after a victory over Chelsea in the final of the Champions League, 2008

scrape through to the quarter-final where a 4-0 home display against Porto, coupled with a goal-less draw in the return, saw them line up a semi-final they lost to eventual Champions Borussia Dortmund.

Many thought 1998 would prove to be United's year as it would be 40 years on from Munich and the 30th anniversary of their previous triumph. Five victories in their group games boded well, but Monaco claimed a semi-final berth on away goals.

United were forced to suffer the ignominy of the qualifying round the following year before they could embark on an unbeaten run through the group stage. They were to face Italian opponents in both the quarter and semi-final games in Inter Milan and Juventus, but held their nerves to book their place in the Final in Barcelona. Bayern Munich took a sixth-minute lead in the Final and it took two last-gasp goals by substitutes Teddy Sheringham and Ole Gunnar Solksjaer to bring the trophy back to Old Trafford on what would have been Sir Matt Busby's 90th birthday.

United have qualified for the knock-out stages for 12 of the last 13 seasons and claimed their third European crown in May 2008. After Ronaldo had headed United into the lead against arch rivals Chelsea in Moscow, Fergie's side could have gone in at half time three goals to the good, had Tevez managed to take his chances. As it was, Lampard equalised shortly before the interval, and extra time failed to separate the two teams. Misses by Ronaldo and Terry in the penalty shootout led to sudden death and, when Van Der Sar saved from Anelka, the trophy was heading for Old Trafford.

Incredibly they very nearly became the first ever side to retain the trophy when they were back in the Final the following year on May 27 2009 in Rome, when they lost to Barcelona falling to goals from Samuel Eto'o and Lionel Messi.

Charity Shield

MANCHESTER UNITED HAVE competed in a record 26 FA Charity Shield matches since its inception in 1908 (when Football League Champions United emerged victorious over Southern League Champions Queen's Park Rangers in a Stamford Bridge replay), winning the trophy on more than half of these new season curtain openers. They have also shared the Shield on four occasions when the match ended in a draw before the introduction of penalty shoot-outs.

United participated in the highest-scoring Shield match when they beat Swindon Town 8-4 in 1911. Alex Stepney was embarrassed when Tottenham goalkeeper Pat Jennings scored against him with a long kick from his own penalty area at Old Trafford in 1967 in a match that finished 3-3.

It was FA Secretary Ted Croker who in 1974 proposed that the Shield should be played at Wembley as a curtain-raiser to the new season between the reigning League Champions and FA Cup holders.

In the 1990s, Manchester United appeared in no fewer than seven Shield matches – winning four (including two on penalties, against Arsenal in 1993 and Chelsea in 1997), drawing one and losing two. The Charity Shield was renamed the FA Community Shield in 2001 and United have continued their love affair with eight appearances already in the first decade of the new millennium.

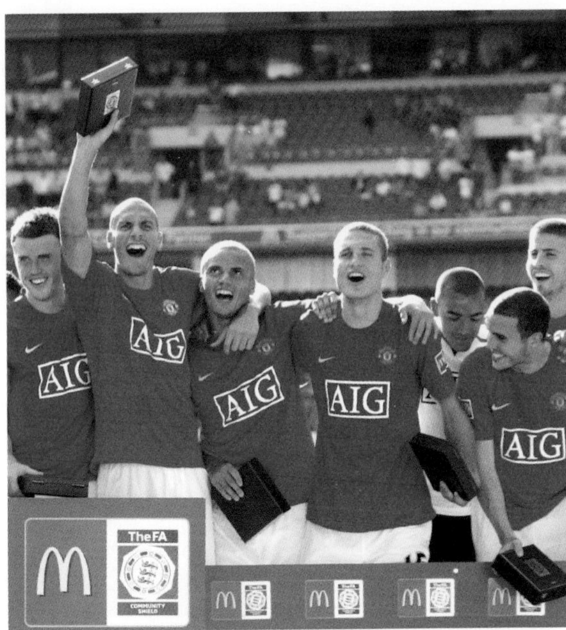

ABOVE Celebrations following victory in the 2007 Community Shield

Charlton

RIGHT Bobby Charlton in action against Spurs

FOOTBALL WAS IN BOBBY Charlton's blood. His mother came from the Milburn soccer family in the northeast with four brothers playing professionally, while her cousin was the legendary Newcastle United's centre-forward Jackie Milburn. Not surprisingly, both her sons took up the game and Jack played for Leeds and England.

Born 11 October 1937 near Newcastle, Bobby Charlton joined United's ground staff in June 1953. As a schoolboy player, it was rumoured that at least 18 clubs wanted to sign him, but he made a promise to join United. His early years saw him score regularly as a reserve, and finally make his debut in October 1956 scoring two goals. He was dropped for the next game to make way for the recently recovered Tommy Taylor.

There was much competition as the Busby Babes started to grow in number and Charlton was only picked to play when various members of the team were injured, notably, Billy Whelan, Taylor or Dennis Viollet. By the end of 1956-57 he was playing more regularly however. With exemplary behaviour both on and off the pitch, Charlton was set to do well with his exceptional eye for the goal. The emerging Babes side enjoyed Championship success with the help of ten goals scored by Charlton during the 1956-57 season. Also at this time he played in the FA Cup team and scored during the semi-final, going on to play in the Final against Aston Villa.

Success eluded the team, but undeterred, Charlton went on to make his European Cup debut against Real Madrid. When their plane crashed at Munich airport on 6 February 1958, eight United players were killed. Charlton escaped serious injury having been dragged unconscious from the wreckage by goalkeeper Harry Gregg. In the following month after the disaster,

Charlton returned to action in the FA Cup sixth round. The team reached the Final, but lost to Bolton. Charlton remained a constant player for Busby, while other players came and went.

The aftermath of the accident was a difficult time for all at Old Trafford and Matt Busby was often in despair. He found in Charlton a great source of inspiration. Charlton, meanwhile, was committed to playing for his club. He made his England debut in April 1958 against Scotland at Hampden Park. He played mostly left-wing and took part in 38 League games, scoring 28 goals, but he didn't feel involved enough. He found his niche in midfield in 1964 where he was able to unleash his creative skills and contribute greatly to Championship success.

Charlton was instrumental in helping England to the World Cup Final in 1966, belting two fine goals past the Portuguese keeper in an earlier game. England won the World Cup in spectacular fashion and Charlton was then voted Footballer of the Year, European Footballer of the Year and Model Player by the referees. In 1968, at the pinnacle of his career, he helped United to their European Cup triumph over Benfica at Wembley.

Bobby Charlton holds the record for most appearances for the club (753 in all competitions) and is the highest goalscorer with 247. Scoring twice in his last ever game for United against Verona at the end of the 1972-73 season, Charlton, having already been awarded an OBE, went on to receive a CBE in January 1974. He was knighted in 1994.

ABOVE Bobby Charlton in action during a match

Coppell

BORN 9 JULY 1955 IN LIVERPOOL, Steve Coppell signed for United in 1975. He had slick ball skills that made him a natural choice for both United and England until injury halted his playing career in 1983.

While studying at Liverpool University, Coppell had joined Third Division Tranmere Rovers, but United's manager, Tommy Docherty spotted his talent and he moved to Old Trafford in early 1975, taking over from winger Willie Morgan. Although his first season ended in losing to Second Division Southampton in the FA Cup Final, United returned to Wembley in May 1977 to defeat Liverpool 2-1, where Coppell picked up the only winner's medal of his career.

In 1981, during an England game, Coppell seriously injured his knee in a tackle with Josef Roth of Hungary. This led to three operations from which he never fully recovered and 14 months later, aged just 28, he was forced to retire from playing professional football. He had played 206 consecutive League games during 1977 and 1981, a United record. He later went on to manage Crystal Palace, Manchester City, Brighton and Reading where he resigned after the final match of the season in 2009 after failing to gain them promotion back to the Premier League.

RIGHT Coppell motivates his teammates during a match, September 1980

Crerand

RENOWNED FOR BEING A TOUGH midfielder, Pat Crerand (born 19 March 1939) signed for United in 1962. He had joined Glasgow Celtic in 1957 at the age of 18. Three months after arriving at Old Trafford, Crerand won the first of many medals including an FA Cup winner's medal against Leicester City in 1963. He quickly established himself as one of United's most constructive midfielders and was known for being an aggressive tackler.

His vision and ability to send the ball long made up for his lack of goals and he became a key member of the United side that won the League Championship in 1965 and 1967 and the European Cup in 1968. Along with Bobby Charlton and Nobby Stiles, Crerand formed one of United's finest ever midfield trios. He had an unquestionable loyalty to Matt Busby and the club and was arguably sometimes too committed, allowing his temper to get the better of him. In a match against Partizan Belgrade in 1966 he was sent off for fighting, but two years later won the European Cup with United against Benfica at Wembley.

During the 1971-72 season, he retired from playing and for a brief time was assistant manager to Tommy Docherty, before becoming manager of Northampton Town in 1976. Crerand's unflinching support for the club and a local radio commentator's job still earn him high regard with supporters.

BELOW Crerand warming up before a game, January 1968

Derbies

BELOW RIGHT Figures correct to end 2008-09 season

BELOW The blue and red halves of Manchester are seperated by stewards and police

THE FIRST EVER MANCHESTER derby took place on 3 October 1891 when Newton Heath beat Ardwick 5-1 in an FA Cup first round qualifier. There have since been more than 130 League and ten Cup meetings between the two local rivals with the red half of Manchester holding the upper hand as the tables below show. Probably the most famous derby match took place on 27 April 1974 when former United favourite Denis Law scored a back-heeled goal for City that would condemn their more illustrious rivals to relegation. Indeed, Law felt so bad that he left the pitch immediately, watching the remaining few minutes from the touchline, and hung up his professional boots.

Although the two sides have met in various rounds of the FA Cup and League Cup, the only showpiece match they have contested was the 1956 FA Charity Shield where League Champions United ran out 1-0 winners against FA Cup holders City thanks to a Dennis Viollet strike. The match was played at Maine Road because the Old Trafford floodlights were not yet operational for this mid-week encounter.

League	Played	Won	Drawn	Lost	For	Against
Man City	140	37	48	53	184	199
Man Utd	140	55	48	37	202	184
FA Cup	**Played**	**Won**	**Drawn**	**Lost**	**For**	**Against**
Man City	7	2	0	5	9	15
Man Utd	7	5	0	2	15	9
League Cup	**Played**	**Won**	**Drawn**	**Lost**	**For**	**Against**
Man City	4	2	1	1	8	4
Man Utd	4	1	1	2	4	8

Docherty

LEFT Tommy Docherty, the Manchester United manager from 1972 to 1977

BEFORE HIS MOVE TO Manchester United in December 1972, Tommy Docherty was a player with Preston and Arsenal, a Scottish international and the manager of Scotland.

Known as 'The Doc', he brought new players to Old Trafford and avoided relegation but this proved to be short-lived, because in April 1974 United were relegated to the Second Division for the first time since 1937. They were Second Division Champions in 1975 and Docherty took his team to the 1976 FA Cup Final where they were beaten by Southampton. Undeterred, United fought back under Docherty's leadership and beat Liverpool 2-1 the following season to claim the trophy.

This was to be Docherty's last match in charge as, when his affair with the club physiotherapist's wife was revealed on 3 June 1977, he lost his job. He continued his career and went on to manage Chelsea, QPR three times, Aston Villa, Rotherham, FC Porto, Derby County, Preston and Wolverhampton Wanderers, ending his career with a short spell in Australia and as manager of non-League Altrincham.

Double

CONSIDERING ONLY THREE TEAMS had previously managed to complete the Double of League title and FA Cup in the 20th century (Tottenham Hotspur in 1961, Arsenal in 1971 and Liverpool in 1986), the fact that Manchester United achieved this feat twice in three seasons underlines their dominance of the domestic game in the 1990s.

Following the capture of their first League title for more than a quarter of a century, United went into the 1993-94 season on a high. By the end of March, they had lost just two League games – both home and away to Chelsea – and would finish the season by suffering just two more defeats to finish with a then-record Premiership points tally of 92. The FA Cup Final saw a 4-0 demolition of Chelsea with Cantona netting two penalties. Sadly, Sir Matt Busby passed away on 20 January so would never see his beloved United register their first Double.

United claimed their second Double in 1995-96, this time losing six games en route to the Premiership title although they remained unbeaten at Old Trafford. Chelsea were the victims in the semi-final this year and it fell to Cantona to score the only goal of the FA Cup Final against Liverpool.

RIGHT United players celebrate victory after the FA Cup Final match against Newcastle United where they completed the Double for the third time in six years, May 1999

FAR RIGHT Cantona and Schmeichel hold the trophy after their FA Cup Final victory against Chelsea at Wembley in 1994. United won the match 4-0 completing their first double

Edwards

RIGHT The legendary Duncan Edwards in January 1958

BORN 1 OCTOBER 1936, DUNCAN Edwards became the youngest ever player in the First Division at the age of just 16. He made his international debut aged 18 for England in the 7-2 victory over Scotland in April 1955, becoming the youngest international player of the 20th century. It is argued that Edwards was the best United player of all time.

By the time of his death, aged 21, in the Munich tragedy, he had earned the nickname 'manboy' because he helped United to win the Youth Cup in the same month that he made his international debut. He won three Youth Cups, two League titles and an FA Cup Finalist's medal.

What made Edwards stand out initially was his size. At 15 he had looked like a giant and played like a man in the opinion of Matt Busby. But he combined awesome power with a lighter touch, he could kill the ball dead and dribble as well as unleashing an accurate 50-yard pass. Edwards was unassuming and liked by his team-mates who just accepted that he could achieve more physically than they could. As left-back, he usually wore the number six shirt, but he was gifted enough to play virtually anywhere on the pitch.

The Busby Babes were a talented bunch, but Edwards was a natural. For 15 days after the Munich crash, he defied chronic kidney damage, a collapsed lung, a broken pelvis and ribs as well as a smashed right thigh before his death on 21 February 1958. Sir Bobby Charlton had the ultimate praise for his former team-mate: "The best player I've ever seen, the best footballer I've ever played with for United or England, and the only player who ever made me feel inferior."

European Cup

ABOVE Action in the Real Madrid goalmouth as United attack

UNITED'S FIRST OUTING IN the European Cup took place on 12 September 1956 when they beat Anderlecht 2-0 away. In the return leg at Maine Road, the home side registered their record European victory with a 10-0 rout. Their run would take them to the semi-final where they lost to holders Real Madrid.

The 1957-58 season saw United again qualify to compete against Europe's elite. This was made more poignant, however, by the Munich air disaster which had occurred as the team were returning home from their victorious quarter-final second leg clash against Red Star Belgrade. The team that beat AC Milan 2-1 in the home leg but lost 4-0 in the San Siro contained just four of the players (Gregg, Foulkes, Morgans and Viollet) whose efforts had got United this far.

It would take until 1965-66 for United to again qualify. They got to the semi-final once more, having defeated the mighty Benfica 8-3 on aggregate in the quarter-final with George Best outshining the newly-crowned European Footballer of the Year Eusebio. But United went out at the hands of Partizan Belgrade.

Their next attempt to claim Europe's top club prize would be successful, however, as Hibernian Malta, Sarajevo and Gornik Zabrze were despatched en route to a semi-final showdown with Real Madrid. Taking a slender 1-0 lead to the Bernabeu, United battled out a 3-3 draw to earn themselves a place in the Final against Benfica. Bobby Charlton (apart from Foulkes, the only Munich survivor in the side) opened the scoring in the second half before Jaime Graca equalised for the Portuguese. Extra time saw three goals from George Best, 19-year-old birthday boy Brian Kidd and a second for Charlton bring the trophy back to England for the first time.

The attempt to retain the trophy began well with a 10-2 aggregate mauling of Irish side Waterford and victories against Anderlecht and Rapid Vienna but AC Milan prevailed.

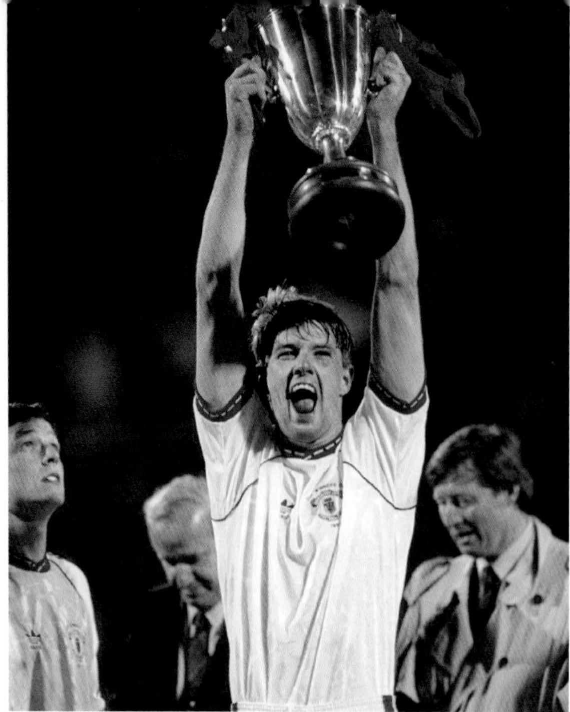

ABOVE Gary Pallister raises the trophy aloft after victory in the European Cup Winners' Cup Final against Barcelona in Rotterdam in 1991

FAR RIGHT European Footballer of the Year, George Best, 1968

European Cup Winners' Cup

UNITED'S FIRST FORAY INTO THE European Cup Winners' Cup came in 1963-64 when they overcame Willem II and Tottenham Hotspur before beating Sporting Lisbon 4-1 at Old Trafford and then losing 5-0 in Portugal to exit the competition. More than a decade would pass before United once again graced the competition, this time registering a victory over St Etienne. They came away from Porto with a 4-0 deficit that they failed to claw back in the return leg, winning 5-2 with goals from Steve Coppell (2) and Jimmy Nicholl and a brace of own goals.

Juventus halted their progress in 1983-84, with United having disposed of Dukla Prague, Spartak Varna and Barcelona in previous rounds. United finally claimed this trophy on 15 May 1991. Having knocked out Pecsi Munkas, Wrexham, Montpellier and Legia Warsaw on their way to the Final, they now came up against Barcelona in Rotterdam. Mark Hughes scored twice in the 2-1 victory against his former club.

United also went on to compete in the European Super Cup as a result and a Brian McClair goal at Old Trafford against Red Star Belgrade gave Alex Ferguson a second European trophy in six months. United's attempt to defend their Cup Winners' Cup title ended with a second-round 4-1 aggregate loss at the hands of Atletico Madrid.

European Footballer of the Year

THAT THREE MANCHESTER United players won the European Footballer of the Year trophy in the space of five years in the 1960s showed that this was no ordinary era for the team and that Law, Charlton and Best were very special talents.

Law was the first of the trio to be honoured after scoring 46 goals in 40 League and Cup games during the 1963-64 season; Charlton was given both the domestic and continental accolade in 1965-66 in helping England to World Cup glory; while Best won the award in 1968 after helping to bring the European Cup to Old Trafford.

The latest Red recipient of the Ballon d'Or, as it is commonly called, is Cristiano Ronaldo who won the award in 2008 again, like Best, after helping United win the European Cup.

FA Cup

RIGHT Cristiano Ronaldo and Glen Johnson of Portsmouth battle for the ball during the FA Cup quarter-final, 2008

MANCHESTER UNITED HAVE won the FA Cup a record 11 times and appeared in 16 Finals (an appearance record they share with Arsenal). Indeed, they are the only club to have appeared in a Final in every decade since the war.

Their debut in the competition ended in a 6-1 first round drubbing at the hands of holders Preston in 1890. Their first taste of success came in 1909 when a Billy Meredith-inspired United emerged victorious with Sandy Turnbull scoring the only goal of the game. It would be almost 40 years before United again graced the Final, this time a 4-2 victory over Blackpool giving Matt Busby his first trophy in 1948.

The late 1950s will be remembered with United finishing twice as runners-up. The first time, in 1957, saw the club hoping to complete the first Double of the century, but a clash with Villa's Peter McParland left keeper Ray Wood with concussion and a fractured cheek-bone. Jackie Blanchflower stood in as his deputy (these were the days before substitutes) but conceded twice as Villa ran out 2-1 winners. The following year, the remnants of the pre-Munich side reached the Final only to lose 2-0 to Bolton Wanderers as Nat Lofthouse bundled Harry Gregg into the net for a controversial goal.

There was only one appearance in the 1960s, a 3-1 win over Leicester City in 1963 before a shock defeat at the hands of Second Division Southampton in 1976. United made amends the following year when they disposed of

Liverpool 2-1 with goals from Stuart Pearson and Jimmy Greenhoff. Arsenal won the 1979 Final with a dramatic late Alan Sunderland goal taking the spoils just a minute after Sammy McIlroy had brought United level.

Two Finals in three years followed, with United overcoming relegated Brighton 4-0 in the 1983 replay after the two sides had played out a 2-2 thriller and dealing Everton's Double hopes a fatal blow two years later. Crystal Palace were the opposition in 1990 when, again after a replay, Alex Ferguson claimed his first trophy as Manchester United manager.

A hat-trick of Final appearances began in 1994 with a 4-0 victory over Chelsea and a 1-0 win over Liverpool sandwiching a 1-0 defeat against Everton. The second leg of the Treble was secured in 1999 with a 2-0 victory over Newcastle United before two more back-to-back appearances.

The 2004 victory over Millwall provided scant compensation for the surrender of the Premiership title to Arsenal. The following year saw the Old Trafford club finish the season empty-handed with Chelsea taking the title and Arsenal claiming the Cup Final on penalties after United had dominated the match. After a fifth round exit in 2006, United reasserted their Cup pedigree by reaching the first Final at the new Wembley in 2007.

ABOVE The team stand on the top deck of a bus surrounded by fans as they parade through Manchester after winning the FA Cup and Premiership Double in May 1996

Famous Fans

THE LIST OF CELEBRITY FANS OF Manchester United is endless but they include, from the music world: Victoria Beckham (former Spice Girl and wife of David), Richard Ashcroft (the Verve), Ian Brown (the Stone Roses), Tim Burgess (the Charlatans), Mick Hucknall (Simply Red), Kym Marsh and opera singer Russell Watson. Former England cricket captain Michael Atherton and snooker player John Virgo *(Big Break)* are two of the many sports stars to follow the Red Devils, as do television personalities Eamonn Holmes (former GMTV presenter), Terry Christian *(The Word)*, comedian Steve Coogan *(Alan Partridge)*, Angus Deayton (the former *Have I Got News For You* host), Patrick Kielty (the Irish comedian who fronted *Fame Academy* and *Celebrity Love Island*), TV chef

RIGHT Opera singer Russell Watson sings before the FA Cup Final, 2002

BELOW TV news presenter Eamonn Holmes is a famous fan

Gary Rhodes and former weather girl turned presenter Ulrika Jonsson. They also attract a multitude of soapstars including *Emmerdale's* Mark Charnock (Marlon Dingle) and Lisa Riley (Mandy Dingle), *Coronation Street's* Michael Le Vell (Kevin Webster) and Sean Wilson (Martin Platt), *EastEnders'* Steve McFadden (Phil Mitchell) and *Dream Team's* Terry Kiely (Fletch) to name a few. Other actors who have proclaimed their loyalty to Old Trafford include James Nesbitt (*Cold Feet* and the voice of *Tractor Tom*) and Christopher Eccleston (the former *Dr Who*).

ABOVE Victoria Beckham, former Spice Girl and wife of David

LEFT Actor James Nesbitt

ABOVE Manchester United celebrate after winning the Premier League, 2009

FA Premiership

HAVING FAILED TO WIN THE FIRST Division title between 1967 and 1992, the inception of the Premier League in 1992-93 saw United claim the trophy at the first attempt and retain it the following year. The final day of the 1995 season arrived with United being in a position to claim a hat-trick of trophies if they beat West Ham United and Blackburn failed to beat Liverpool. As it turned out, Blackburn lost at Anfield but United could only manage a 1-1 draw at Upton Park so the title went to Ewood Park.

With Eric Cantona reinstated to the side following his eight-month ban, United began to reel in Kevin Keegan's Newcastle United side that had amassed a seemingly unassailable lead at the top of the Premiership. A 1-0 victory at St James' Park in March 1997 brought the gap to one point and proved a turning point as the Magpies finished the season in second place, four points adrift.

United finished second to Arsenal in 1997-98 but then went on to win three consecutive Premierships before their dominance faded.

Chelsea again dominated the 2006 campaign but United went on to complete another hat-trick of Premier League wins on May 16 2009, when they secured their 11th Premier League title – and 18th League title overall – following a 0-0 draw at home to Arsenal.

Ferdinand

AFTER HIS TALENTS AS AN accomplished defender in the 2002 World Cup were made evident, Alex Ferguson decided that Rio Ferdinand (born 7 November 1978) was just what United needed to sort out their shaky defence. He was transferred from West Ham United for the record fee for a defender of £30 million and signed for United in July 2002.

Ferdinand is renowned for his calm ability on the ball, his talent for maintaining great pace and his aerial flair. Armed with good organisational skills and his talent to anticipate the game, Ferdinand has established himself as one of the world's top defenders. He only really found his feet at United towards the end of his first season, after injury and lack of form hampered his efforts at the start, and he helped United win their 15th League title.

In September 2003, Ferdinand missed a routine drugs test and despite appealing was banned for eight months in January 2004. He was the team's defensive lynchpin and with Ferdinand's ban firmly in place, United finished the season in third.

ABOVE Rio Ferdinand clears as AS Roma forward Mirko Vucinic looks on during their Champions League match, April 2008

A stalwart of both the United (more than 300 appearances) and England (72 caps) defence, he signed a new five-year contract in May 2008. Six days later he went on to captain United to Champions League glory in Moscow. It was a fitting way to end a near flawless season for the centre-back. His good form continued into the 2008-09 campaign, with Ferdinand playing a crucial role in United's record-breaking clean-sheet run.

ABOVE Sir Alex Ferguson receives his manager of the month award, April 2008

FAR RIGHT Sir Alex in hairdryer mode, April 2006

Ferguson

ALEX FERGUSON SECURED HIS status as one of the most successful managers in the history of the game following his move to Manchester United in November 1986.

After a playing career as a centre-forward including a spell at Rangers, Ferguson brought his skills and determination to football management. He stayed at East Stirling for three months before being offered the managerial post at St Mirren where within 18 months he turned the team around and actively encouraged crowds to come and see his team play. Ferguson then moved to Aberdeen where he broke the dominance of Celtic and Rangers in Scottish football, claiming three domestic League titles, four Scottish Cups, the European Cup Winners' Cup and a Scottish League Cup.

In 1986, having been Scotland's caretaker manager for the World Cup in Mexico, he arrived at Old Trafford. His first few seasons proved difficult and he managed three unsuccessful campaigns before United won the FA Cup in 1990. Ferguson realised that success had eluded the team simply because United had become used to Cup runs. With that in mind, he began to change his players and the departures involved Neil Webb, Jesper Olsen, Mark Robins and Paul McGrath, while newcomers included Steve Bruce, Gary Pallister, Peter Schmeichel, and Paul Ince.

Ferguson's second triumph was the European Cup Winners' Cup in 1991. Changes were also taking place in the youth system which was to grant significant results, but the most significant change of all was probably the arrival of Eric Cantona. Criticised for his choice of player, Ferguson knew that Cantona was his lynchpin. His decision was proved right when United won the 1992-93 Premiership. This was followed by the Double in 1994 and domination of English football.

Fans were shocked by Ferguson's decision to sell Hughes, Kanchelskis and Ince, but he was confident in the youngsters coming through the ranks, who included Beckham, Scholes, and Ryan Giggs. In 1999 Ferguson led his team to an unprecedented Treble by winning the Premiership, the FA Cup and the European Cup. The achievement saw Ferguson become the first working manager to be knighted – and, despite an attempt at retirement, his career and enthusiasm show no signs of

slowing down with a current haul of 11 Premiership titles, five FA Cups, three League Cups, two Champions League crowns and a FIFA World Club Cup in 2008.

Foulkes

FOR 18 SEASONS, BILL FOULKES (born 5 January 1932), was the rock at the heart of United's defence. He arrived at United in 1950, making his League debut against Liverpool in December 1952. He had convinced Matt Busby of his fitness for the game, although in fact he had an ankle injury which affected his appearances for the remainder of the season.

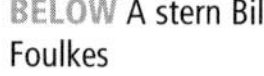

BELOW A stern Bill Foulkes

Playing at full-back, Foulkes was a regular member of the Busby Babes and was one of the survivors of the Munich air crash. Two weeks later, along with Harry Gregg, he was playing against Sheffield Wednesday in the fifth round of the FA Cup. Like Bobby Charlton, Foulkes was instrumental to Matt Busby's rebuilding of the United team and his manager put him in the centre-half position.

Bill Foulkes went on to score a spectacular goal in the semi-final of the 1968 European Cup against Real Madrid. His goal sent United to the Final, where the team beat Benfica 4-1. After Munich, it was an emotional time for those who had survived. United had rebuilt their shattered team and the consistent contributions made by Foulkes had been rewarded with European victory.

Giggs

BORN ON 29 NOVEMBER 1973, RYAN Giggs was just 17 when he made his debut in the first team as a substitute against Everton in the 1990-91 season. As a winger, he has the ability to run with the ball at lightning speed, which added to his sense of balance, ensures he gives the opposition plenty to worry about. Ten years later, he was the youngest ever United player to receive a testimonial.

During his second season with the club in 1991-92, Lee Sharpe's injuries enabled Giggs to earn a regular first-team place where he played an important role in United's League Cup win. It was also in this season that he was capped for Wales, becoming their youngest international. In 1992 he also received the PFA Young Player of the Year award and captained United's youth team to victory in the FA Youth Cup. The following year saw him again awarded with the PFA Young Player of the Year, becoming the first player to win it twice.

His fame was spreading and his image was used in merchandise from

ABOVE Ryan Giggs tangles with Jason Roberts of Blackburn Rovers, 2008

ABOVE Giggs passes Peter Sweeney of Millwall during the 2004 FA Cup Final at the Millennium Stadium

T-shirts to Quorn burgers. In 1994, aged just 20 he published his autobiography, while on the pitch he continued to shine, helping United to secure the League and FA Cup Double in 1993-94 season and win the double Double two years later.

Giggs collected his fourth FA Cup winner's medal in 2003-04 and his 11th Premiership medal in 2008-09. In amongst all the statistics and games for the club, his sensational winning goal against Arsenal in the 1999 FA Cup semi-final replay remains the fans' favourite memory of this living legend.

In the Champions League Final against Chelsea, Giggs overtook Bobby Charlton's long-standing record with his 759th appearance for United and he has now gone on to surpass 800 games for his only club. His longevity was recognised by his peers in 2009 when he won the PFA Players' Player of the Year award.

Glazer

BORN IN ROCHESTER, NEW YORK in 1928, Malcolm Glazer's self-made wealth was estimated to be $1 billion in 2004. This is a far cry from his life when in 1943 he took over the running of his late father's shop. Ever the entrepreneur he began investing money in mobile home parks during the 1970s, but the 1980s brought failed bids for businesses such as Harley-Davidson, although he did successfully buy the virtually bankrupt oil company Zapata, founded by former President of the US, George Bush.

Three of his sons run the Tampa Bay Buccaneers which he bought for $192 million, but after winning the Super Bowl in 2003, the team's worth soared and it took $8 million to hire coach Jon Gruden. Since 2003, Glazer has been building up a sizeable stake in United, but fans were hostile to his interests in the club.

Glazer now has control of the club and has installed his sons Joel, Avram and Bryan on the board. Oldest son, Avram is credited with formulating his father's £790 million takeover of United.

BELOW Joel, Avram and Bryan Glazer, sons of owner Malcolm Glazer, are seen before the Champions League third qualifying round

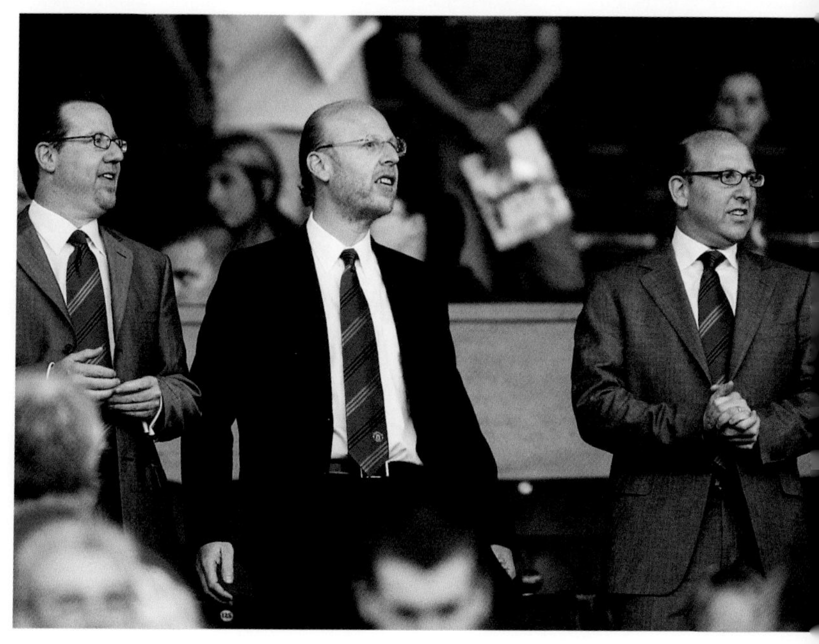

Greatest XI

Manager
Sir Alex Ferguson

1	Peter Schmeichel
2	Duncan Edwards
3	Bill Foulkes
4	Steve Bruce
5	John Carey
6	Bobby Charlton
7	David Beckham
8	Eric Cantona
9	Ryan Giggs
10	George Best
11	Denis Law

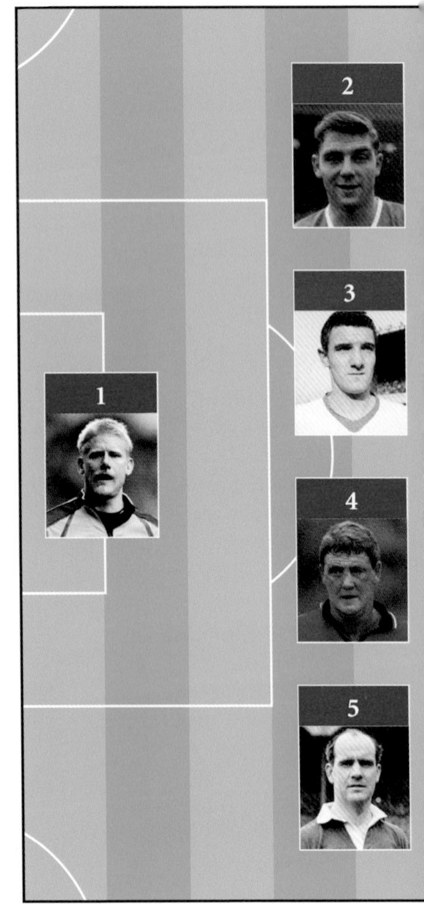

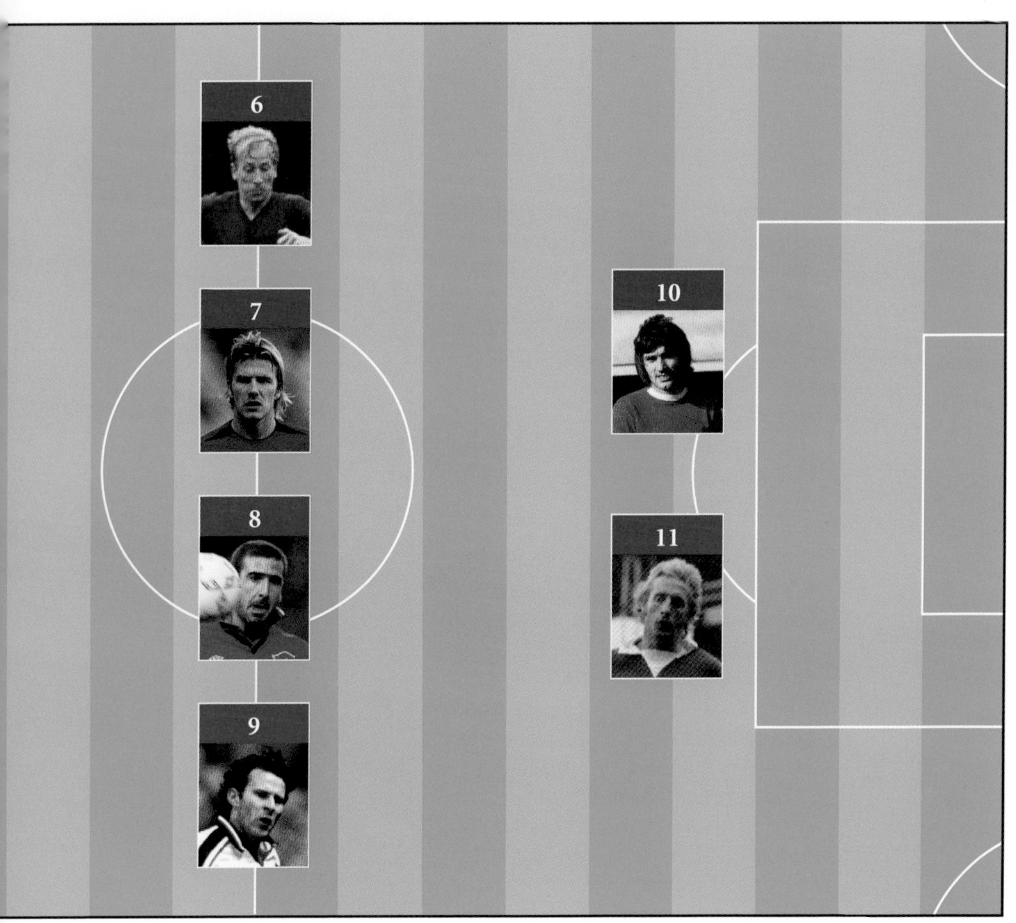
6
7
8
9
10
11

Greenhoff

BROTHERS BRIAN (BORN 28 APRIL 1953) and Jimmy (born 19 June 1946) Greenhoff joined United in 1973 and 1976 respectively. Brian established himself as a midfielder while older brother Jimmy played in a forward position. Brian switched to centre-half after the 1974-75 season, playing alongside Martin Buchan in the FA Cup Finals of 1976 and 1977. He was rewarded for his efforts with England caps at full, 'B' and Under-23 levels.

Jimmy joined his younger brother at United from Stoke City when the club's flagging fortunes needed his inspiration. Despite being 30 when he signed in November 1976, he had impeccable ball control and the ability to score spectacular goals. He struck up a formidable partnership with fellow striker Stuart Pearson. During the 1977 FA Cup Final, Jimmy scored the winning goal against Liverpool, but found himself on the losing side in the Final two years later.

He left United in December 1980 and went on to join Crewe and Toronto Blizzard, making the last of his more than 650 League appearances in December 1983 with Rochdale.

RIGHT Brian Greenhoff (centre) lifting the FA Cup with his brother Jimmy who scored Manchester United's second and winning goal in the final against Liverpool at Wembley

STER UNITED

Hargreaves

BELOW Owen Hargreaves in action for United

IN HIS OWN WORDS, IT WAS "POSsibly the longest-running transfer saga" in the history of football. But after several months of prolonged pursuit, United finally signed Owen Hargreaves from Bayern Munich in May 2007 for a fee of around £17 million.

The Canadian-born, England international midfielder's stock had risen dramatically in the previous year, and by the time he arrived at Old Trafford, he had become one of European football's most highly thought of defensive midfielders, having won four Bundesliga titles with Bayern.

After an injury-disrupted start to his United career, Hargreaves came to the fore in the second half of the successful 2007-08 campaign with a string of tireless and confident performances in midfield and also, on occasion, at right-back. He capped a satisfying debut season with a superb penalty in the Champions League Final shoot-out victory over Chelsea. But a recurrence of his knee problem – and a subsequent operation in the USA – forced Owen to miss almost all of the following season.

Born and raised in Calgary, Canada, Owen left for Germany aged 16 to join Bayern Munich. Success was quick as Bayern claimed both the 2000-01 Bundesliga title and the Champions League crown. Hargreaves remains one of only two English players to win the European Cup with a non-English club – the other being Steve McManaman.

The following season witnessed Hargreaves' breakthrough at international level. He would have been eligible to play for Germany or Canada, but opted for England and played his first full international in 2001. Initially a squad player, it took until the 2006 World Cup in Germany for Hargreaves to truly be seen as a key man, and he was voted England Player of the Year in January 2007.

Hargreaves brings vast experience to United's midfield, as well as a determined, energetic and enthusiastic style which gives a well-balanced feel to United's engine room.

Hughes

ABOVE Mark Hughes celebrates after scoring the third goal in the FA Cup Final against Chelsea in 1994

MARK HUGHES, BORN 1 NOVEMBER 1963, enjoyed two spells at United from 1983-86 and 1988-95. His flamboyant playing style delighted fans while his ability to win matches made him valued by his managers. He signed as a professional with United in November 1980 after five months as an apprentice. As a schoolboy player, United's youth coach Syd Owen changed his position from midfielder to centre-forward. He made his League Cup debut in November 1983 when Ron Atkinson gave the Welshman his first-team opportunity. During the 1984-85 season, Hughes was voted PFA Young Player of the Year.

In 1986, given the opportunity by Atkinson, he decided to sign for Barcelona, but his form suffered and he only managed one goal in 17 games. Hughes didn't settle in Spain and only scored four goals in 28 games. He was then loaned to Bayern Munich where he rekindled his love of football. Atkinson, who had not been forgiven for selling Hughes, was replaced by Alex Ferguson in 1986. Hughes was what Ferguson needed and he re-signed him for £1.5 million in 1988.

In 1989, 'Sparky' was voted Player of the Year, then in 1991 he became the first player to win the PFA Player of the Year award twice. He went on to win a second FA Cup winner's medal, the European Cup Winners' Cup against former team Barcelona and the League Cup. He formed a great alliance with Eric Cantona on his arrival in 1992 which helped United to their first League title for 26 years.

In January 1995, the arrival of Andy Cole marked the end of Hughes' time at United and he left for Chelsea for £1.5 million. He has since become a successful manager although fans are not best pleased that he is now the boss of arch rivals Manchester City.

Ince

RIGHT Paul Ince in action against Barcelona in the Champions League

OPPOSITE Mark Jones, one of the Busby Babes

PAUL INCE, BORN 21 October 1967, provided United with its driving force in midfield during the early 1990s. He arrived in 1989 from West Ham United for £2 million. As a 21-year-old he had talent which was to develop over the six seasons he played for the club. His maturity enabled him to captain England, and he was the first black player to captain for his country in a match against the United States, and he is only the fourth United player to captain an international game. In just one season he had gone from England debut to captain.

Partnered by Roy Keane in midfield, Ince maintained his tremendous form to be part of the team that won the Double in 1994. He had an incredible ability to run with the ball, setting up the attack for his team-mates, while his tackling skills frequently stopped the opposition. His departure from Old Trafford in June 1995 came as a shock, but Alex Ferguson thought that in his last season for the club Ince had under-performed. When Inter Milan offered a record £7 million for the player, his manager decided to let him go.

Ince has now turned his skills to managership and having cut his teeth at Macclesfield went on to manage Blackburn Rovers before being given the chop in the 2008-09 season.

Jones

MARK JONES, BORN 15 JUNE 1937, was just 17 when he made his United debut in 1950. Outside of football, Jones was renowned for his pipe-smoking and raising budgies which, alongside his impressive physical appearance, gave the impression of maturity beyond his years.

He joined the first team during the 1954-55 season, where as centre-half he created a formidable barrier for the opposition. He was renowned for keeping the ball on the move with simple but effective play and for passing the ball quickly. Matt Busby admired and valued his young player but Jones had to share his centre-half position with his friend and team-mate Jackie Blanchflower, whose skills were much in demand. Both players were products of the club's youth system.

Jones, one of the eight United players to be killed at Munich, was 24 when he died.

Jordan

RIGHT Striker Joe Jordan playing in the third round of the FA Cup at Spurs, January 1980

BORN IN SCOTLAND ON 15 December 1951, Joe 'Jaws' Jordan intimidated opposing defenders with his direct and physical approach. Jordan was an international player for his country, gaining 52 caps. It was his winning goal that took Scotland to the World Cup Finals for the first time in 16 years in 1974.

After a successful career at Leeds, United signed him for more than £380,000 in 1978, a record fee at the time. As a strong and tall player, his skill and aerial ability made him a fearsome forward. In his time at Old Trafford he made 125 appearances and scored 41 goals. In 1981, Jordan left United to join AC Milan, before joining Verona. He later played for Southampton and Bristol City before taking up management positions at Bristol City, Heart of Midlothian and Celtic where he was assistant manager.

He had a long spell as coach at Portsmouth and when manager Harry Redknapp left to become manager of Tottenham Hotspur, he followed him to the club signing in November 2008.

Keane

ROY KEANE WAS BORN 10 AUGUST 1971 and started his career at United in 1993 signing for £3.75 million from Nottingham Forest. Already a Republic of Ireland international, Keane proved his worth immediately, scoring two goals on his home debut as United beat Sheffield Wednesday 3-0. He was able to celebrate the end of his first season with a League and Cup Double.

He established himself in midfield after the departure of Paul Ince at the end of the 1994-95 season and helped United become double Double winners the following year. He succeeded Eric Cantona as captain in 1997, but a cruciate ligament injury kept Keane out for most of the 1997-98 season. The following season saw Keane back in action, however, and his powerful tackling, exceptional passing and his ability to motivate his team-mates when he felt their standards were slipping were evident as he captained United to the Premiership title and the FA Cup as well as the European Cup.

In the European Cup semi-final second leg against Juventus, United were 2-0 down and in need of inspiration.

ABOVE Roy Keane during the Premier League match between United and Blackburn, April 2005

ABOVE Keane wins the Football Writers' Association Footballer of the Year award, May 2000

Keane's header brought United in with a chance as the score became 2-1, but he failed to give up and his encouragement of the team ensured them a 3-2 victory. United were in the Final for the first time in three decades, but he disappointingly missed it through a suspension. Nicknamed 'Massive' by the fans, Keane was awarded the Football Writers' Association Footballer of the Year award in 2000 along with the Professional Footballers' Association award.

After a short spell at Celtic, he took Sunderland to the Premiership in his first management post. He has since walked out on the club and now manages Ipswich.

Kidd

BORN ON 29 MAY 1949, BRIAN KIDD was a keen United supporter whose dreams came true when he signed schoolboy forms at the age of 14. He went on to sign apprentice forms before signing professionally for the team at the start of what was to be a fine career.

Kidd showed excellent form in United's reserve side and Matt Busby rewarded him with a debut at the start of the 1967-68 season in the Charity Shield when he went on as substitute for the injured David Herd. His impressive form ensured him of a regular first-team place – he only missed four matches during his first season.

On 29 May 1968, Kidd's 19th birthday, he played in United's European Cup Final victory over Benfica, scoring the third of United's four goals. As a tribute from fans, the Beatles classic 'Hello, Goodbye' was sung with the chorus words changed to "Eusebio, and I say Kiddo." Despite being capped for England twice, Kidd's only honour at United was that European Cup medal and he moved to Arsenal for £110,000 after United's relegation to the Second Division in 1974. His career was further enhanced by moves to Manchester City, Everton and Bolton Wanderers, before he rejoined Manchester United after spearheading the Professional Footballers' Association initiative to encourage clubs to work more closely with the community.

He eventually took over the youth development project and in 1991 became assistant manager to Alex Ferguson before an ill-fated sojourn as manager at Blackburn Rovers in the late 1990s. Varied backroom management positions have followed including an assistant's role to manager Paul Hart at Portsmouth during the latter part of the 2009 season.

ABOVE Brian Kidd in action against Benfica in the 1968 European Cup Final

RIGHT Martin Sullivan, CEO of AIG, poses with Ji-Sung Park (L), Wayne Rooney (2nd from left), Cristiano Ronaldo (2nd from right) and Gary Neville (R) after announcing the club's new shirt sponsors in 2006

MIDDLE Steve Bruce, models the 1992 away shirt

FAR RIGHT TOP A group of shirts bearing the names and numbers of famous Manchester United players from the '90s

FAR RIGHT BOTTOM Bryan Robson in the 1990 away shirt

Kits

ALTHOUGH EVERYBODY TODAY associates Manchester United with red shirts, Newton Heath started their League career in shirts with red and white quarters and blue shorts. For ten years, they switched between this, white shirts and blue shorts and green and gold shirts. With chairman John Davies, came the red shirts that have now become a tradition. The basic red shirt did not dramatically change for years – although the club did experiment with a white shirt bearing a V around the neck and maroon shirts with white hoops during the 1920 and 1930s.

The shirts did not include an emblem on the chest until 1973, although badges were added for special occasions including FA Cup Finals. A badge depicting a phoenix rising from the ashes was added for the 1958 Cup Final held just three months after Munich. Replica kits were first made available to supporters in 1977 and sponsors' names appeared on the shirts in 1983.

The club has gone back to the future with its latest first-team kit. A black 'v-shape' stripe features on the shirt's chest together with a black round-neck collar – reminiscent of shirts worn by Manchester United during the 1908-09 season, when they reached the FA Cup Final.

The shirts still carry the logo of AIG, the American insurance giants, whose contract with the Premier League champions expires at the end of the 2009-10 season.

Law

RIGHT Denis Law takes a penalty during a match against West Ham United at Upton Park in 1970

COMBATIVE SCOT DENIS LAW'S flair for being in the right place at the right time matched with his lightning football brain made 'the King' a prolific goalscorer over his 11 years at Old Trafford.

His early career saw him play for Aberdeen schoolboys, where his slim build and slight squint conspired against him, but this may also explain his aggressive style of play. As he was unable to wear his glasses on the pitch he played with his right eye shut. He soon attracted the attention of Archie Beattie, whose brother Andy was manager of Huddersfield Town where he was taken on as an apprentice in 1955. An operation cured his squint which gave him sight, though slightly blurred, in his right eye.

Matt Busby spotted Law (born 24 February 1940) in an FA Youth Cup tie against United and he offered Huddersfield £10,000 for him. The offer was rejected and Law went on to make his League debut for Huddersfield aged 16. Matt Busby, then manager of Scotland, capped Law against Wales in 1958 where he scored in a 3-0 win. After short spells for Manchester City and Torino, Law arrived at United in 1962. He quickly earned himself honours during the 1960s but missed out on the European Cup Final through injury.

After 236 goals in 399 games for United, new manager Tommy Docherty believed Law had peaked and gave him a free transfer at the end of the 1972-73 season. He moved back to Manchester City and scored the goal that consigned United to the Second Division in 1974. He retired from football that year at the age of 34.

League Championship

UNITED PREDECESSORS NEWTON Heath joined an expanded First Division in 1892 and endured a torrid two-year stay in the top flight, winning just six games out of 30 in each season, although they did register their record League victory, 10-1 against Wolves in October 1892. A 12-year spell in the Second Division ended in 1906 and United went on to enjoy a successful period for the rest of that decade. Mid-table mediocrity was then the norm until relegation in 1922.

The situation was dire on 5 May 1934 when United travelled to Millwall needing to win to avoid relegation to the Third Division (North) for the first time in their history. A 2-0 victory was achieved and two years later they clinched the Second Division title to claim a place in the top flight.

The club has played in the top division of English football since 1938 with the exception of the 1974-75 season. The club was a founding member of the Premier League in 1992, and after winning the Championship for the third time in a row in 2008-09, now holds the joint record for the most English League titles with 18.

ABOVE Sir Alex Ferguson and captain Roy Keane hold the Premiership trophy

ABOVE Alex Ferguson leads out the team to celebrate being crowned FA Carling Premier League Champions, 2001

League Cup

PRIOR TO FACING WIGAN IN THE 2006 Final, Manchester United had won the Football League Cup just once since its inaugural 1960-61 season. That was in 1992, when a Brian McClair goal beat Nottingham Forest 1-0 to claim the Rumbelows Cup (the trophy has also been known as the Worthington Cup, Milk Cup, Coca-Cola Cup and Carling Cup in its various incarnations).

It took them until 1982-83 to register their first appearance in the Final and their opponents were Liverpool, who were three-quarters of the way through a four-year domination of the competition. Although United took the lead through Norman Whiteside, Liverpool fought back to claim an extra-time victory. The Old Trafford side have been runners-up on two other occasions, losing to former manager Ron Atkinson's charges each time. In 1990-91 United registered their highest away win in the competition when they demolished Arsenal 6-2 at Highbury en route to a Wembley meeting with Sheffield Wednesday. The Owls managed just one shot on target during the whole 90 minutes and John Sheridan's strike proved decisive.

Three years later, United fell at the final hurdle to Aston Villa who took a 2-0 lead before Mark Hughes pulled one back with eight minutes remaining. Andrei Kanchelskis handled the ball in the last minute and Dean Saunders calmly stroked the ball past Les Sealey to seal a 3-1 win.

The 2006 Final victory over Wigan was something of a canter with two goals from Rooney and strikes from Saha and Ronaldo securing a 4-0 win, while they added the 2009 League Cup to their trophy cabinet, after defeating Spurs 4-1 on penalties.

ABOVE United players celebrate winning the Carling Cup after defeating Wigan Athletic in the Final at The Millenium Stadium, 2006

League Positions

ABOVE Gary Neville celebrates being crowned FA Carling Premier League Champions in 2001

Season Ending	Division	Position
1892-93	Division 1	16
1893-94	Division 1	16
1894-95	Division 2	3
1895-96	Division 2	6
1896-97	Division 2	2
1897-98	Division 2	4
1898-99	Division 2	4
1899-1900	Division 2	4
1900-01	Division 2	10
1901-02	Division 2	15
1902-03	Division 2	5
1903-04	Division 2	3
1904-05	Division 2	3
1905-06	Division 2	2
1906-07	Division 1	8
1907-08	Division 1	1
1908-09	Division 1	13
1909-10	Division 1	5
1910-11	Division 1	1
1911-12	Division 1	13
1912-13	Division 1	4
1913-14	Division 1	14
1914-15	Division 1	18
1919-20	Division 1	12
1920-21	Division 1	13
1921-22	Division 1	22
1922-23	Division 2	4
1923-24	Division 2	14
1924-25	Division 2	2
1925-26	Division 1	9
1926-27	Division 1	15
1927-28	Division 1	18
1928-29	Division 1	12
1929-30	Division 1	17
1930-31	Division 1	22
1931-32	Division 2	12
1932-33	Division 2	6
1933-34	Division 2	20
1934-35	Division 2	5
1935-36	Division 2	1
1936-37	Division 1	21
1937-38	Division 2	2
1938-39	Division 1	14
1946-47	Division 1	2
1947-48	Division 1	2
1948-49	Division 1	2
1949-50	Division 1	4
1950-51	Division 1	2
1951-52	Division 1	1
1952-53	Division 1	8
1953-54	Division 1	4
1954-55	Division 1	5
1955-56	Division 1	1
1956-57	Division 1	1
1957-58	Division 1	9
1958-59	Division 1	2

1959-60	Division 1	7
1960-61	Division 1	7
1961-62	Division 1	15
1962-63	Division 1	19
1963-64	Division 1	2
1964-65	Division 1	1
1965-66	Division 1	4
1966-67	Division 1	1
1967-68	Division 1	2
1968-69	Division 1	11
1969-70	Division 1	8
1970-71	Division 1	8
1971-72	Division 1	8
1972-73	Division 1	18
1973-74	Division 1	21
1974-75	Division 2	1
1975-76	Division 1	3
1976-77	Division 1	6
1977-78	Division 1	10
1978-79	Division 1	9
1979-80	Division 1	2
1980-81	Division 1	8
1981-82	Division 1	3
1982-83	Division 1	3
1983-84	Division 1	4
1984-85	Division 1	4
1985-86	Division 1	4
1986-87	Division 1	11
1987-88	Division 1	2
1988-89	Division 1	11
1989-90	Division 1	13
1990-91	Division 1	6
1991-92	Division 1	2
1992-93	Premier League	1
1993-94	Premier League	1
1994-95	Premier League	2
1995-96	Premier League	1
1996-97	Premier League	1
1997-98	Premier League	2
1998-99	Premier League	1
1999-2000	Premier League	1
2000-01	Premier League	1
2001-02	Premier League	3
2002-03	Premier League	1
2003-04	Premier League	3
2004-05	Premier League	3
2005-06	Premier League	2
2006-07	Premier League	1
2007-08	Premier League	1
2008-09	Premier League	1

ABOVE Manchester United footballers, (from left) Bobby Charlton, Denis Law, George Best and Billy Foulkes celebrating after winning the League Championship 1967

League Title

BELOW United players celebrate after Denis Law scores his club's third goal against Arsenal to become Division One Champions at Old Trafford, 1965

MANCHESTER UNITED HAVE won the Division One title on seven occasions, the first coming in 1907-08, only their second season back in the top flight, with a team including the inspirational Billy Meredith and Charlie Roberts. A further title followed in 1910-11 but the club would then have to wait 40 years before reclaiming the trophy.

The 1950s heralded a new era for the club with the introduction of the Busby Babes. Roger Byrne was the first of these youngsters to make his debut, in November 1951, and he contributed vital goals as United clinched the 1951-52 title. Back-to-back Championships were claimed between 1955 and 1957 when the likes of Bobby Charlton and Duncan Edwards swept all before them.

In 1955-56, Dennis Viollet scored 20 League goals as they lost just seven times, finishing 11 points clear of second placed Blackpool. The following year saw them win 28 games, losing just six times (three away and three home) but events in Munich tore the promising team apart. The final two titles of the pre-Premiership era arrived in the 1964-65 and 1966-67 with a side fronted by the awesome attacking force of Charlton, Law and Best.

Managers

THE TWO MANAGERS THAT stand out and who have contributed more than any of the other 13 managers are Sir Matt Busby and Sir Alex Ferguson. Both tireless in their efforts to gain the best out of their respective teams, they each reaped the rewards of effort and determination with their personal best wins. For Matt Busby, winning the 1968 European Cup was a triumph, while for Alex Ferguson it is winning the Treble in 1999.

It all began with Ernest Mangnall's (1903-12) building of the new stadium at Old Trafford in 1910. He resigned from United and moved to Manchester City where he was again responsible for building a new stadium (Maine Road). Under his leadership United won promotion to the First Division in 1905-06 and won the FA Cup for the first time in 1909. Mangnall was replaced by John Robson in 1914 and despite World War I, Robson's team remained in the First Division but were relegated after his departure when he was succeeded by John Chapman in 1921.

Chapman endured a disappointing first season with United, but enjoyed promotion three years later when they went on to the FA Cup semi-finals, but were dashed by Mangnall's Manchester City. In 1926, due to misdemeanours that were never made public, Chapman was suspended by the FA and he made way for Clarence Hilditch (1926-27). As United's first ever player-manager, Hilditch's time at United was brief, returning to his playing role.

He was succeeded by Herbert Bamlett (1927-31), who had originally been a referee. His career as manager was not as successful as that of a referee and he was replaced by Walter

ABOVE Alex Ferguson watches from the bench during the Celtic v United Tom Boyd Testimonial at Celtic Park, May 2001

Crickmer (1931-32), who never officially became manager, but took charge of team affairs twice during his 38-year career as secretary. In 1932, Scott Duncan began his five years at Old Trafford. Despite his experience as a player, Duncan never really made it as a manager and their position at the time was, and still is, United's lowest ever League position.

BELOW Sir Matt Busby with the European Cup, July 1968

The club was without a manager until Matt Busby arrived in 1945. He was assisted by Jimmy Murphy who played an enormous part in rebuilding the team after the 1958 Munich disaster. Wilf McGuiness (1969-70) took over for six months following Matt Busby's retirement, but was quickly succeeded by Frank O'Farrell, the only Irishman to manage the club. He was dismissed after the team's bad form in the 1972-73 season.

Tommy Docherty (1972-77) was replaced by Dave Sexton (1977-81) who had previously replaced him at both Chelsea and Queen's Park Rangers. Injuries to the team in 1980 caused poor results and Sexton's services were no longer required. Ron Atkinson took over in 1981, but again, due to poor form, the manager was replaced and Sir Alex Ferguson began his illustrious career with United in November 1986.

McGuinness

ORIGINALLY A BUSBY BABE, WILF McGuinness's playing career was cut short when he broke his leg badly in a reserve match against Stoke City in 1960, forcing retirement at the age of 22. McGuiness, born 25 October 1937, became youth team manager in 1961 and became senior coach when Matt Busby announced his retirement in 1969.

A year later he was appointed manager but only held the post for six months. He returned to coaching the reserves for the following 12 months but then decided to take up a position as coach in Greek football to Aris Salonika and the Panachaiki Patras. He returned to England to manage York City, before spells with Hull City and Bury before retiring from football in 1992. He was a qualified physiotherapist and is currently an in-demand after-dinner speaker.

LEFT Wilf McGuiness, pictured when a United player, went on to manage the club

McIlroy

RIGHT Busby's final signing, McIlroy in action for United, September 1978

MATT BUSBY'S FINAL SIGNING IN September 1969 was Samuel Baxter McIlroy, born 2 August 1954. The young player was a big United fan and George Best, a fellow Belfast lad, was his hero. McIlroy made a dramatic first-team debut for United three months after signing as a professional. The match was against Manchester City at Maine Road and he scored his first goal as a professional in front of a crowd of 63,000, having a hand in the other two in a thrilling 3-3 draw.

He was the third youngest player to be given an international cap, playing for Northern Ireland against Spain at the age of 17. After being seriously injured in a car crash in January 1973, he missed many games of the following season, but quickly established himself as a first team regular during 1973-74. Unfortunately, the team was relegated during that season but McIlroy bounced back with the side that won the Second Division Championship at the first attempt. By this time, he was also playing regularly for Northern Ireland, giving a resourceful performance as a midfielder while notching up an impressive goalscoring record.

He appeared in three FA Cup Finals for United and later collected a winner's medal when United defeated Liverpool at Wembley in 1977. In October 1981, he was dropped from the first team to make way for newly-signed Bryan Robson but he responded by scoring a hat-trick against Wolverhampton Wanderers. McIlroy made more than 400 appearances for United before being sold to Stoke City in 1982. He moved back to Manchester to join City three years later after a very short spell at Bury.

McIlroy clocked up 88 caps for Northern Ireland before he retired from playing. He subsequently managed several English football teams and the national team, gaining most success with Macclesfield Town. He is currently the manager of Football League Two side Morecambe.

Megastore

IN THE EAST STAND AT OLD TRAFFORD lies the Megastore. Spread over a monumental 18,000 square feet, the Megastore boasts that it is the biggest shop devoted to football to be found. There are some incredible interactive features including TV screens showing the team in action to a huge screen where promotional clips from any of the videos on sale can be watched.

On each pillar throughout the store famous players who wore the number seven are represented by a huge picture, including Bryan Robson, Steve Coppell and Eric Cantona – obviously, there are more recent holders such as David Beckham and Cristiano Ronaldo.

The Megastore is open every day, but hours are limited on matchdays. The Megastore sells virtually anything you can think of from mugs, scarves, away shirts, Nike training and leisurewear to women's clothes and replica shirts.

BELOW The Manchester United Football Club Megastore

Meredith

A GIANT OF THE GAME DURING the late 1890s and early 1900s, Billy Meredith joined United in 1906. As a slightly framed man, the Welshman, born 30 July 1874 and nicknamed 'Old Skinny', did not give the appearance of a footballer. However, his skills and his ability on the pitch gave him celebrity status long before being a celebrity was common.

BELOW Billy Meredith in action during the first ever FA Charity Shield match against Queens Park Rangers in 1908

He was renowned for playing with a toothpick sticking out of his mouth which he said helped him to concentrate – in fact, a newspaper cutting from 1909 claimed he was unable to play without it. Before joining United, Meredith was suspended in 1905 during his time at Manchester City for allegedly bribing an Aston Villa player. Meredith denied the charge but other financial irregularities were then found at Hyde Road and the FA dismissed several directors and banned several players for 12 months.

Although his ban was quashed in December 1906, Meredith had already been transferred to United and he played an instrumental part in turning them into one of the top clubs of the time. United won the League Championship in 1908 and 1911. In 1907, the Players' Union was formed. Meredith and other team-mates were under great pressure from the FA to disassociate themselves from the newly-formed body, but Meredith refused to conform and continued his association by joining several other United players and training independently for the 1909-10 season. They were known as 'The Outcasts'. Eventually the FA relented and an agreement was reached allowing the Union to be acknowledged. For Billy Meredith, this was one of his finest victories.

At the grand age of 47, Meredith retired from United after becoming increasingly disenchanted with the club. He re-signed for Manchester City as player and coach for a further three years, appearing in the FA Cup semi-final against Newcastle United at the age of 49.

Mitten

BORN IN BURMA ON 17 JANUARY 1921, Charlie Mitten joined United in 1936 and signed professional two years later, but he was to be with the club for nearly ten years before he made his full League debut. World War II began almost as soon as he signed and he worked as an RAF physical training instructor around Britain's aerodromes, but he was able to keep up his football and made guest appearances for clubs such as Chelsea and Tranmere Rovers.

In 1946, he made his debut for United under the guidance of Matt Busby, newly installed as manager. Occupying the left-wing position, Mitten was a pillar around whom Busby built his classic post-war side. Mitten's speed and shooting ability were an essential ingredient to success in the FA Cup triumph of 1948 and the following season his continued skill contributed to 23 goals in League and Cup games for the club.

In 1950 while touring in the US and Canada, several United players were approached by Colombian clubs, offering lucrative contracts. Mitten decided to go, and since Colombia was not a member of FIFA he was able to join Santa Fe FC, but within a year, his new nation had joined FIFA and he was obliged to return to an unforgiving Matt Busby. His decision cost him £250 and a six month suspension, whereupon he was transferred to Fulham for £20,000.

BELOW Mitten scores despite the best efforts of Wolves goalkeeper Bert Williams, March 1949

Munich Air Disaster

THE UNITED PLAYERS WERE ON their way home from a European Cup quarter-final against Red Star Belgrade. On 6 February 1958, their plane stopped at Munich airport to refuel, a routine procedure that should have taken no longer than 20 minutes. What was to follow cost the lives of 21 people, including eight United players and three members of staff along with journalists, supporters and associates.

After a night of celebrations following the match in Belgrade, the Busby Babes boarded the Elizabethan class AS 57, 'The Lord Burghley', bound for home. The chartered plane was piloted by Captain James Thain and his friend and co-pilot Captain Kenneth Rayment. Captain Rayment was scheduled to pilot the plane even though Captain Thain was in command. As the plane reached Munich airport for the scheduled stop the passengers noticed it was snowing. As refuelling was not going to take long the passengers remained on board and at 2.31 pm with full tanks, Flight 609 received clearance to take off.

The plane picked up speed but the pilots could hear an odd note from the engines and take-off was aborted after 40 seconds. Both pilots agreed that the noise they heard was the result of 'boost-surging', caused by rich fuel making the engines over-accelerate. This was not uncommon in this type of plane and the pilots saw no reason for alarm. To compensate, the pilots let the throttle out more slowly and again attempted take off. The problem remained and the pilots decided to taxi back to the terminal and discuss what to do. The passengers were informed of a technical fault and asked to disembark.

While several passengers discussed the possibility of travelling overland or taking the Hook of Holland sea route, Duncan Edwards sent his landlady a telegram stating that he would be home the following day. He was wrong in his assumption that their flight was cancelled and the passengers were recalled. After consultation, the two captains had decided against an overnight stay in Munich in order to retune the engines and as the problem seemed confined to the port engine and the plane was able

to take off with a single engine they were satisfied it was possible to leave the ground safely.

On its third attempt to leave the runway many of the passengers were frightened. Johnny Berry actually voiced his concern that they were all about to be killed, with devout Catholic Liam Whelan answering that he was ready to die. Just as the plane was about to take off it burst off the runway at high speed, skidding through a fence before it shot off across a road. After colliding with a house, which tore off a wing, the cockpit hit a tree while the body of the plane hit a hut full of tyres and fuel, causing the plane to explode with flames.

Harry Gregg became a hero by freeing himself from the wreckage and then rescuing a crying baby and her mother who had suffered a fractured skull and legs. He dragged Dennis Viollet and Bobby Charlton clear. By this time, Matt Busby was on the ground, while Jackie Blanchflower was lying badly injured. The stewardess was paralysed with shock. At last cars and trucks arrived at the crash scene. Passengers were rushed to the Rechts der Isar hospital in Munich. Matt Busby was to stay in hospital for 71 days, twice having the last rites administered, before being allowed home to Manchester and Jimmy Murphy was left to pick up the pieces.

The eight players who died were: Geoff Bent, full-back (25); Roger Byrne, full-back (28); Eddie Colman, half-back (21); Duncan Edwards, half-back (22) – he survived for 15 days after the crash; Mark Jones, half-back (24); David Pegg, forward (22); Tommy Taylor, forward, (26) and Liam Whelan, forward (22), while the members of staff who perished include: Walter Crickmer, club secretary; Tom Curry, trainer and Bert Whalley, coach.

ABOVE An official from British European Airways' Munich office with firemen beside the wreckage of the BEA Elizabethan airliner

Neville

ABOVE Phil (L) and Gary Neville in action during training with Manchester United at Soldier Fields, during a US tour, July 2004

GARY NEVILLE BELONGS TO AN elite group of players who have skippered the club to the Premier League title. Following on from Bryan Robson, Steve Bruce, Eric Cantona and Roy Keane, Neville realised a lifelong dream as he became the fifth United captain to lift the Premier League trophy following the club's record ninth triumph at the end of the 2006-07 campaign.

Neville himself had missed the final stages of the campaign, having suffered ankle ligament damage just 11 minutes into the visit of Bolton to Old Trafford on 17 March 2007. The same injury kept the Reds' skipper out for most of the 2007-08 season but even when unable to influence matters directly on the pitch, his presence is felt in the dressing room and from the stands. Nobody wants United to win more than Gary Neville.

The defender, who has made more than 560 appearances in a United shirt scoring seven goals since graduating from the youth team, was handed the armband during the 2005-06 season following Roy Keane's departure. Being one of United's most consistent and committed performers since establishing himself in the side in 1994-95 at the expense of Paul Parker, Neville was a natural choice and to this day he still enters every game refusing to contemplate defeat. He also has 85 England caps but has yet to score an international goal.

His younger brother Phil Neville, born 21 January 1977, joined United as a trainee in 1993, breaking into the first team alongside Beckham in 1995. He struggled to maintain a regular first-team place, despite his abilities as both a full-back and midfielder. He has six Premiership titles, three FA Cups, a Champions League winner's medal and a World Club Cup title. His performances for United, including eight goals, saw Phil win more than 50 caps for England. In a surprise move the younger Neville moved along the East Lancs Road to join Everton in August 2005 for a reported £3.5 million.

Newton Heath

RAILWAY MEN FROM PICCADILLY Station in Manchester formed a team made up of men from the carriage and wagon department of the Lancashire and Yorkshire Railway at Newton Heath. They formed the team, named Newton Heath LYR, in 1878 establishing themselves at a ground near the railway yard.

First games were often against other railway men and when the Football League was formed in 1888 the team did not think they were good enough to compete. Despite their lack of confidence, the team began to dominate local competitions and slowly began to look for games that could equal their talents. In 1890, Newton Heath applied to join the Football League, but without success, only gaining one vote. Undeterred, they formed an organisation called the Football Alliance and campaigned alongside other clubs to impress the Football League. After a further three applications they were eventually accepted in 1892.

The League had a reshuffle where the First Division was expanded, and included Newton Heath and the Second Division was born. Local rivals, Ardwick (later to become Manchester City), joined the Second Division. Newton Heath's career was neither exciting nor distinguished but after many and ups and downs, including times when the team was almost disbanded and debts totalled £2,600, Manchester United Football Club was born in 1902.

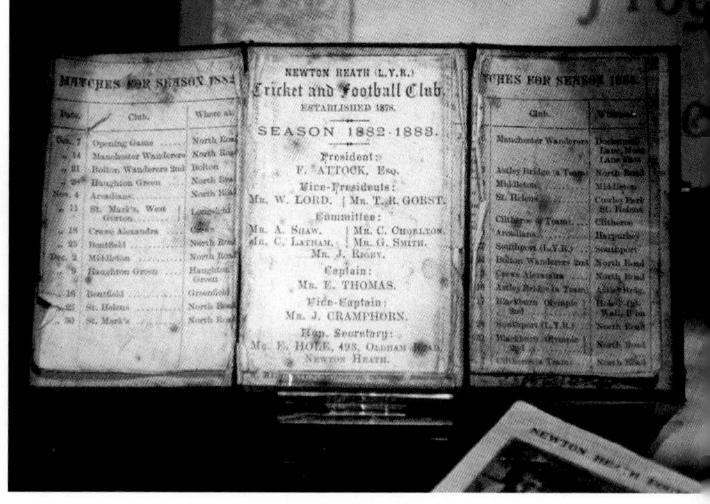

BELOW A Newton Heath fixture list from 1882-83

Nicknames

THE GIVING OF A NICKNAME HAD a special status in Viking society in that it created a relationship between the name maker and the recipient of the nickname but Matt Busby was alleged to have disliked the term bestowed on his Busby Babes because he thought it cast aspersions on their youth. He preferred instead to label his youngsters the Red Devils. This term is now the club's nickname and is immediately identifiable all over the world.

The media was quick to label Alex Ferguson's crop of youngsters that dominated the Premiership in the 1990s Fergie's Fledglings. The stadium's nickname has also become synonymous with Manchester United after former hero Sir Bobby Charlton labelled Old Trafford the Theatre of Dreams.

It is not just the club, the ground or a set of players who have received nicknames over the years. Several individuals can be easily recognised by their alternatives. United have had two Kings (Denis Law and Eric Cantona) gracing the hallowed turf along with a Guv'nor (Paul Ince) and Captain Marvel (Bryan Robson), to name but a few.

BELOW The Red Devil, symbol of Manchester United

Old Trafford

AFTER THE CLUB WON ITS FIRST FA Cup in 1909, John Davies paid £60,000 for a site close to the Old Trafford cricket ground. The new stadium was designed by respected Scottish architect Archibald Leitch and was built with the likelihood of extension in mind.

Old Trafford's first match saw United play host to Liverpool on 19 February 1910 with VIP invitations boasting the new ground could accommodate 100,000 fans. A roof was erected over the United Road terrace in 1934 but bomb damage suffered during the Second World War prompted the redevelopment that began the creation of today's stadium.

United played their home games at neighbouring Maine Road while the ground was rebuilt. The Main Stand was covered in 1951 and the Stretford End in 1959 while March 1957 saw the floodlights turned on for the first time. The ground benefited from improvement in the mid-1960s to bring a 58,000-capacity in time for the 1966 World Cup. After the Taylor Report, the terraces disappeared from the Stretford End in 1993 with the away end soon suffering the same fate which reduced the capacity to 44,000. Between 1995 and 2000, capacity was increased to 68,000.

The stadium was chosen as a venue for the 1996 European Championships and hosted its first European Cup Final in 2003. Work has taken place to extend the capacity to approximately 76,000 by filling in the corners of the North East and North West corners and by adding an additional tier to link the North Stand with the East and Stretford Ends. Future expansion is likely to involve the addition of a second tier to the South Stand, which would raise the capacity to over 90,000.

ABOVE Inside Old Trafford, home of Manchester United

BELOW External view of Old Trafford

One Hundred Club

ABOVE Ruud van Nistleroy celebrates in front of stunned Southampton fans with team-mates Ryan Giggs and Wayne Rooney after scoring the goal that condemned Southampton to relegation at the St. Mary's Stadium, 2005

RIGHT Goals scored in all competitions to end 2008-09

Player	Dates played	Goals
Bobby Charlton	1956-73	249
Denis Law	1962-73	237
Jack Rowley	1937-55	211
George Best	1963-74	179
Dennis Viollet	1952-62	179
Joe Spence	1919-33	168
Mark Hughes	1983-86, 1988-95	163
Ruud van Nistelrooy	2001-2006	150
Ryan Giggs	1991-	148
Stan Pearson	1937-54	148
David Herd	1961-68	145
Paul Scholes	1994-	142
Tommy Taylor	1953-58	131
Brian McClair	1987-98	127
Ole Gunnar Solskjaer	1996-2007	126
Andy Cole	1995-2001	121
Cristiano Ronaldo	2003-2009	118
Sandy Turnbull	1906-15	101
Joe Cassidy	1895-1902	100
George Wall	1906-15	100

Pallister

BEGINNING HIS CAREER IN NON-League football with Billingham Town, Gary Pallister, born 30 June 1965, went on to become one of United's most successful players. Even when playing for Billingham, Pallister was working 16-hour shifts on Teesside Docks. In April 1988, while playing for Middlesbrough, he became one of the few players to be capped for England while playing outside the top division.

Signing for United in 1989, Pallister was a tall, commanding central defender who built a strong partnership with Steve Bruce. Their formidable alliance began on Pallister's signing and lasted until 1996, while between 1990 and 1992 their understanding for each other's game enabled them to win a hat-trick of Cup successes.

Pallister signed for the club for the record fee of £2.3 million and Alex Ferguson had high hopes for him. He recognised potential in Pallister and, after a shaky start where he conceded a penalty on his debut, put the mighty man on a rigorous training regime which built up muscle and turned Pallister at 6ft 4in into a giant. The triumphs and Cup victories gave United the chance and the confidence for a run of four Premiership titles in five years.

Missing only one game between 1992 and 1995, Pallister played over 400 times for United in all competitions, combining consistency with a fast pace and comfort with the ball. He received very few bookings during his career and was only once sent off which the FA later agreed was an error. During the 1995-96 season, he was forced to miss many games due to back problems, but managed to return for the climatic end to the season when United won their second Premiership and FA Cup Double.

Not known for his goalscoring, the two goals he headed into the net against Liverpool at Anfield undoubtedly won United the Premiership and Pallister received his fourth Premiership winners' medal. Back trouble again intervened and he finally moved back to Middlesbrough in July 1998 for £2.5 million.

BELOW Gary Pallister lifts the Premier League trophy after their 3-1 win over Blackburn Rovers at Old Trafford, May 1993

Pegg

RIGHT David Pegg in action, February 1957

IT TOOK DIPLOMACY ON the part of United's chief scout, Joe Armstrong to encourage David Pegg (born 20 September 1935) to sign for the club in 1952, aged 16. Pegg was the most sought-after schoolboy player, having earned five England schoolboy caps.

He was a naturally gifted winger who worked in real contrast to right-winger Johnny Berry. Berry was renowned for his direct approach and his ability to dart in and out of the opposition's territory, while Pegg was adept at swerving and fluid movement. But he also had the ability to cut inside suddenly and was most powerful close up with a left foot that could kick the ball with great force through the opposition defence.

He made his debut for United in December 1952 against Middlesbrough, but his position in the first team was not secure and he constantly battled with Albert Scanlon for the left-wing position. Matt Busby, had at the time, a team that was bursting with talent, but Pegg's performances in the FA Youth Cup saw victories in 1954 and 1956 and did much to enhance the image of the Busby Babes. David Pegg was a reserve at the time of the Munich air crash and sadly did not survive the tragedy.

ABOVE Cristiano Ronaldo who came third in the Player of the Year award

Player of the Year

AWARDED SINCE 1974, MEMBERS of the PFA, the players union, vote on who has been the best player. All professional footballers, regardless of nationality, under the age of 23 playing in the English leagues are eligible for the Young Player of the Year award and, the following Manchester United players have been recipients: Mark Hughes (1985), Lee Sharpe (1992), Ryan Giggs (1993 and 1994), David Beckham

PLAYER OF THE YEAR

ABOVE Cristiano Ronaldo was PFA Player (and Young Player) of the Year in 2007 and 2008

(1997, Wayne Rooney (2005), Cristiano Ronaldo (2007 and 2008) and Ryan Giggs (2009). Recipients of the Player of the Year award are: Mark Hughes (1989 and 1991), Gary Pallister (1992), Eric Cantona (1994), Roy Keane (2000), Teddy Sheringham (2001), Ruud van Nistelrooy (2002) and Cristiano Ronaldo (2007 and 2008).

The Football Writers' Association have since 1948 presented an annual award to the player whom its members deem the best football player in England. The following United players have been honoured: Johnny Carey (1949), Bobby Charlton (1966), George Best (1968), Eric Cantona (1996), Roy Keane (2000), Teddy Sheringham (2001) and yet again Cristiano Ronaldo (2007 and 2008).

Quinton

A STAY AT TOTTENHAM HOTSPUR as a junior did not lead to success as a senior for Quinton Fortune who then moved to Atletico Madrid to try his luck. Born 21 May 1977, his native South Africa gave him an international debut against Kenya in 1996 when he impressed the South African manager and played for the 'B' team.

He joined United in 1999 for £1.5 million and was admired for his attacking play in midfield. He scored four goals in six matches making a good start with his new team and scored another against South Melbourne in the Maracana stadium in the World Club Championship. By the end of the 2002 World Cup, Quinton had aroused interest from other clubs and he was linked with moves to Japan and Italy. He signed a new three-year contract with United at the end of the 2002-03 season, but suffered a broken leg (not realising for a week he had broken it), at Anfield on 1 December which restricted his appearances.

Quinton has earned 53 caps for South Africa including playing in the 1998 and 2002 World Cups. After leaving United, he had short spells at Bolton and Sunderland but is currently unattached.

ABOVE Quinton Fortune and Nigel Quashie of Southampton battle for the ball during the Premiership match between Southampton and Manchester United in May 2004

Roberts

ABOVE United captain Charlie Roberts before their match against Arsenal in 1912

CHARLIE ROBERTS, BORN 6 APRIL 1883, became one of United's all time influential captains. Signing for the club in 1903, his transfer fee from Grimsby Town was £600. The meagre fee for such a phenomenal player was to turn out to be a great bargain for United and Roberts quickly became Ernest Mangnall's right-hand man on the field. He made his debut in 1904 and for the following nine seasons was rarely out of the first team. Playing in the centre-back position he established himself in the United defence.

Roberts, Dick Duckworth and Alex Bell contributed to one of the most outstanding half-back line-ups of all time. He captained a side that won League Championships in 1908 and 1911 as well as taking United to lift the FA Cup for the first time in 1909. As a founding member of the Football Union, Roberts – alongside Billy Meredith – held strong in his principles and did not allow the FA to persuade him to denounce the newly formed Union.

Even though new clauses in players' contracts demanded that they renounce the Union, Roberts decided to fight, whereupon he was suspended by the FA. Like Meredith and several other United players, Roberts became one of 'The Outcasts' and began training independently for the 1909-10 season. When the FA were forced to reassess their position and players were allowed to return just hours before the beginning of the season, Roberts was able to go back to the job he did best, captaining the strong United side.

After nine years at United he was transferred to Oldham Athletic aged 30 and he went on to captain his new side to second place in the League Championship during the 1914-15 season. His fight for the Players' Union may have cost Roberts the opportunity of caps for England, as he gained only three, but Northern Ireland chose him to represent them nine times.

Robson

ONLY FIVE PLAYERS HAVE EVER played for England more times than Bryan Robson and only two have captained the national team more than he did. For nearly ten years, Robson led United and England, collecting 90 caps and six trophies. A win against Barcelona in the 1984 European Cup Winners' Cup quarter-final where he scored two goals showed him at his best.

Born on 11 January 1957, Robson started his career aged 15 with West Bromwich Albion. At 5ft 2in, weighing only 7 stone he was small, but according to his then manager Don Howe showed character and inner confidence. He was put on a diet of Guinness and raw eggs which helped to build him up and he made his professional debut for Albion in April 1975. In the following season he played 16 times and the club won promotion. But Robson broke his leg three times during his first season and still managed eight goals in 23 appearances.

At Albion, Ron Atkinson was the manager under whom he worked best and the team went on to reach the UEFA Cup quarter-final beating Manchester United 5-3 at Old Trafford. After Atkinson moved to United, he managed to persuade Robson to join him so he could build a team around him to challenge Liverpool's domination. He made his debut for United at Tottenham in October 1981 four days after signing for the club for a record £1.5 million. He had made his debut for England a year earlier when they played the Republic of Ireland.

During 1982, while Kevin Keegan was out through injury, Robson became England's most influential player and Bobby Robson, the England manager (1982-90), was Robson's biggest fan, giving him the name of 'Captain Marvel'. Later that same year, Atkinson made him captain of United and he led the team to the 1983 FA Cup. In 1994 after several lean years with United, Robson was offered a coaching role at United but chose instead to head into management with Middlesbrough and later Bradford City and WBA.

ABOVE Bryan Robson celebrates another United victory

Ronaldo

BELOW Cristiano battles with Barcelona's Rafael Marquez during the UEFA Champions League semi-final, April 2008

LOVE HIM OR LOATHE HIS theatrical antics, there is little doubt that Cristiano Ronaldo was one of the best players ever to pull on the famous red shirt.

In six years at Old Trafford, the Portuguese winger exhausted all superlatives as he matured from the inexperienced youngster who left Sporting Lisbon in 2003 to become arguably the best footballer on the planet.

The story goes that Sir Alex was persuaded to buy Ronaldo – largely unknown when he signed as an 18-year-old for £12.24 million in 2003 – by his players on the plane home from a pre-season friendly against Sporting. In his first season for the club, Ronaldo made 39 appearances and scored eight goals including one in the FA Cup Final against Millwall and was named the Sir Matt Busby Player of the Year.

On the international scene, he was one of the few Portuguese players who emerged from Euro 2004 with their reputation enhanced, while he survived an unseemly spat with clubmate Wayne Rooney in the following World Cup to become United's star of the 2006-07 season. That all paled into relative insignificance, however, compared with his achievements in the following campaign.

Taking the world by storm, Ronaldo scored 42 goals as United were supreme during 2007-08. His magical 2008 was rounded off with another string of individual honours. In October he was named Player of the Year, and in December became the first United player since George Best in 1968 to be awarded the prestigious Ballon d'Or trophy. To cap it off, in January 2009, he became the first Red to win the FIFA World Player of the Year award.

In his final appearance of the 2008-09 season at Old Trafford, Ronaldo received his third Championship medal after the Reds sealed the title with a point against Arsenal. At that stage, there was no indication that Cristiano was contemplating an exit – but that all changed less than a month later when the club announced it had accepted Real Madrid's world record £80 million offer.

ABOVE Rooney in action in the Premier League, 2008

Rooney

WAYNE ROONEY JOINED UNITED on 31 August 2004, transferring from Everton for a fee that could eventually reach £30 million. His League debut was against Spurs at Goodison Park at the start of the 2002-03 season, and nine games in he scored his first Premiership goal at the age of 16 in Everton's 2-1 victory over Arsenal.

With exceptional talents quickly spotted at international level, Rooney, born 24 October 1985, became England's youngest ever player in February

BELOW Rooney in the Champions League, September 2004

2003 when he was brought on as a substitute against Australia at Upton Park. He became the youngest player to score for his country when aged just 17 he netted a goal in September 2003 against Macedonia. He further impressed for England at the European Championships in Portugal in 2004 where he scored four goals in four games. but his preparations for the 2006 World Cup were hampered by a broken metatarsal and his form didn't live up to expectations.

Sir Alex Ferguson had been watching Rooney since he was 14 and it was at this point that he decided he needed to sign the young striker, who made his debut for the club on 28 September 2004 against Fenerbahce. He scored twice in that match to endear himself to the United fans and would finish the season as the club's top scorer with 17 goals in all competitions.

Over the following five years he notched 236 appearances scoring 97 goals. But it's not just Wayne's goals that have endeared him to the United faithful. A tireless worker, he always gives 100 per cent and can't stand losing. They're traits that have, from time to time, landed him in hot water but Reds fans recognise the odd over-zealous challenge or act of petulance is merely a by-product of Rooney's immense passion and will to win.

Rowley

ABOVE Alf Ramsey (right) of Spurs tussles for the ball with Jack Rowley of Manchester United during their match at White Hart Lane, September 1953

AT THE AGE OF 17, IN ONLY HIS second appearance for United, Jack Rowley scored four goals in a League match against Swansea Town. Born 7 October 1920 in Wolverhampton, Rowley signed for United in 1937. As centre-forward, he proved he was a true professional having been spotted by Major Frank Buckley who never actually played him for the first team at Wolverhampton Wanderers.

He moved to Bournemouth and scored ten goals in his first 11 matches but was quickly signed by United who paid £3,000 for him. Like other players during World War II, Rowley missed around six seasons while on active service having joined the South Staffordshire Regiment. At the start of the war, League football was not played, but the government soon realised it was good for public morale and professional players then in service were actively encouraged to play for the League club they were nearest to.

Ironically, Rowley guested for Wolves and scored eight goals in the match, but making a guest appearance for Tottenham in 1944 proved memorable when he topped their goalscoring list and helped them win the League South title. He also played for England that same year and was given an assignment in the front line at the D-Day Normandy landings.

He returned to Old Trafford and became United's leading goalscorer during the 1945-46 season with 20 goals in 28 matches. During his 422 appearances for the club he scored 208 times. He moved to Plymouth Argyle in 1955 to become player-manager.

Schmeichel

AGED 20, PETER SCHMEICHEL (BORN 18 December 1963), began his career at the Danish club of Hvidovre, where his talent was soon spotted by the Danish Premier side Brondby, who signed him in January 1987. At 6ft 4in, Schmeichel was a huge presence in goal and one of the tallest goalkeepers in League football. He was voted Danish Player of the Year in 1990 and became the best goalkeeper in European football. United were determined to sign him and Alex Ferguson got his man in August 1991 for the modest fee of £500,000.

In his first season he conceded only 33 goals in 42 League games which was the lowest number that season and, when United defeated Nottingham Forest at Wembley, Schmeichel received a League Cup winner's medal for the 1-0 victory. Schmeichel was happy at United and stated he would be with the club 'for life'. The start to the 1992-93 season was not promising for Schmeichel who conceded six goals in the first three games, but he went on to keep five consecutive clean sheets between August and September. continuing to excel as he did so.

It was having Schmeichel in goal that enabled United to end their 26-year wait for the Championship and in February 1993 he was presented with the Premier League's Goalkeeper of the Year award. Only 31 goals made it past him in the entire season. During the following season, his ability to throw powerfully to the likes of Giggs and Sharpe and the fact he conceded very few goals allowed United to enjoy a Double-winning campaign. His penalty save from David Seaman against Arsenal in August ensured victory for United in the Charity Shield.

LEFT Schmeichel watches action during the FA Cup Final against Chelsea at Wembley, 1994

However, in the FA Cup quarter-final he was sent off and missed the League Cup Final defeat to Aston Villa. Up to his suspension, he managed to play in a total of 94 consecutive games which is the longest ever run for a United goalkeeper.

His goal was virtually untouched during the 1994-95 season but the following season was to show him at his best. In ten League games he only conceded seven goals which helped United to the Premiership title for the third time in four years. He enjoyed a fourth Championship medal at the end of the 1996-97 season when his outstanding contributions also included a save from a header by Rene Wagner that already appeared to be in the goal. It turned the tables for United who were, by Schmeichel's actions, then able to secure a place in the quarter-final of the Champions League. In September 1995 he was voted European Goalkeeper of the Year.

He won a winner's medal with Denmark in Euro '96 and was voted Carling Player of the Year in August. Representing his country yet again in 1998, Denmark reached the quarter-final of the World Cup. Schmeichel, renowned for kicking both goalposts before a match for luck, decided to quit Old Trafford after the 1998-99 Treble.

Scholes

RIGHT Scholes during a match against Aston Villa, Old Trafford 2008

PART OF THE NEW WAVE of talent that ushered in Beckham, Giggs, Butt and the Neville brothers in the mid-1990s, Salford-born Scholes scored twice on his debut in the League Cup at Port Vale in 1994-95 – and on his first League outing against Ipswich – and hasn't looked back.

A host of golden seasons at Old Trafford include 1995-96's Double-winning campaign, in which he covered admirably during Eric Cantona's suspension, finishing second behind the Frenchman in the scoring charts with 14 goals; he was a cornerstone of 1999's Treble-winners, although suspension ruled him out of the UEFA Champions League Final; and in United's Premier League success in 2003, his 20-goal haul was vital.

Neat and compact, a misplaced Scholes pass remains one of the rarest sights in football. His superb eye for goal and late runs from midfield also served his country superbly on 66 occasions.

An eye problem kept the man the fans dubbed the 'Ginger Prince' out of action for a large part of 2005-06, but he burst back onto the scene during the 2006-07 title-winning campaign, playing a key role in helping the Reds reclaim the Premier League crown.

His good form continued the following season as he helped the club to a glorious Double and finally buried the Champions League ghost of '99 when his stunning strike against Barcelona in April 2008, booked United's, and his own place, in the Final in Moscow.

Now in the top four highest ever appearance makers, with over 600 games under his belt, and in the top 12 highest goalscorers at the club, Scholes is, indisputably, one of the finest talents in United's history, and he's still going strong with a contract taking him through to June 2010.

BELOW Scholes nets for United against Sunderland

Stepney

RIGHT Alex Stepney pictured in September 1975

ALEX STEPNEY WAS born 18 September 1942 and enjoyed a career at Old Trafford from 1966 to 1978. He became the top-scoring goalkeeper for the club when he converted two penalties in the 1973-74 season. Matt Busby was to say that "The single most important factor behind our Championship success in 1967 was signing Alex Stepney".

Not renowned for being a spectacular player, Stepney provided reliability and proved steady and efficient. His sense of anticipation and positioning was a rarity that was a bonus to the club. He was goalkeeper at a time when the club enjoyed enormous success, including the European Cup in 1968, where Stepney made an outstanding contribution by saving from Eusebio and United carried away the trophy, beating Benfica. Originally transferred from Chelsea for £55,000, Stepney, from south London, had already won three England Under-23 caps. He showed promise at a time when Matt Busby needed to strengthen his goalkeeping position.

Tommy Docherty, then manager of Chelsea, decided to let Stepney go after only five months with the club and he proved a key factor in United's League Championship of 1966-67, playing in every game. Chosen 20 times as a substitute for England, he only ever managed one full cap, against Sweden.

Stiles

ABOVE Nobby Stiles pictured in December 1969

NORBERT 'NOBBY' STILES had no less than 28 England caps during his career. With United between 1960 and 1971, he won League Championship winner's medals in 1965 and 1967, and a World Cup winner's medal in 1966 followed by a European Cup winner's medal in 1968. In 14 years and nearly 400 appearances, Stiles, having signed for the club professionally in 1959, was thrown into first-team action making his debut in October 1960 against Bolton Wanderers.

Born 18 May 1942, Stiles had been an avid fan of United since a schoolboy and the local lad from Collyhurst established himself as a regular, making 31 appearances during his first season. His tackling was fierce and he was known for his aggressive style on the pitch which made him a permanent midfield fixture with the added bonus of being able to defend when necessary. His fitness levels were unique and he also hammered home goals when needed.

International recognition came for Stiles at the right time and in his first full-capped season he played no less than eight times, going on to figure in all England's World Cup matches. He will be remembered for his jig around Wembley when England celebrated victory against West Germany in a 4-2 win.

Stretford End

THE STRETFORD END IS WHERE every Manchester United fan would like to sit to watch every home game. Situated opposite the Scoreboard End, the first cantilevered stand was built in 1964 at a cost of £350,000 but the current structure – completed almost 30 years later and boasting a 400-capacity banqueting suite – has a price tag of over £10 million. Since the changing rooms were built in 1993, the players emerge from the corner of the pitch by the Stretford End.

RIGHT A view of the Stretford End at Old Trafford

BELOW A view from the Stretford End with giant inflatable footballs suspended from the roof prior to the 2003 UEFA Champions League Final

MUFC
REPUBLIC OF MANCUNIA
RED ARMY
MBRO

Supporters' Club

SUPPORTERS OF UNITED CAN BE found worldwide. Although United have always enjoyed a 'big club' status in British football, it was the Munich air disaster that was to give the club its high profile throughout the world. It is the best-supported club in English football with huge attendances at home games while their away following is renowned for being one of the loudest in the country. The capacity of Old Trafford has just risen to 76,000, yet there are more than 140,000 members of the club.

There are 200 affiliated branches of the Manchester United Supporters' Club, the majority of which are UK based. United continues to enjoy strong support from Ireland with whom it has long had an affinity and small Irish towns regularly arrange travel to United games in England. One of the largest Supporters' clubs is based in Scandinavia, while other countries with branches include the US, Mauritius, South Africa and Iceland.

BELOW Malaysian Manchester United Football Club supporters hold a football signed for them by the Queen, left, and another signed by the Duke Of Edinburgh

Taylor

ONE OF THE BUSBY BABES, TOMMY Taylor (born 29 January 1932) signed for United in March 1953, making his debut at Old Trafford against Preston North End and scoring two goals. He was a talented youngster who had deputised for his uncle in a local pub team as centre-forward at the age of 16. He had started playing football some years earlier as left-back, playing only further forward when the school team was short of players.

He signed amateur forms at Barnsley in 1948, signing professionally for the club a year later. He made his debut in the first team in the Paisley Charity Football Cup in 1950 with his first League game against Grimsby later that same year. During national service, Taylor's football career was in jeopardy when he cracked a bone, tore ligaments and suffered severe cartilage damage. But a year out of the game and two operations later, Taylor was able to return to Barnsley.

Tommy opted to play for United rather than Cardiff City after 26 goals and 44 appearances for Barnsley when the Second Division team needed to sell him for financial reasons. United was not too far away from his Barnsley home and Taylor, described by Alfredo di Stefano as 'Magnifico', used his lightning speed, thunderous shots and powerful headers to become one of United's greatest goalscorers of all time.

After just ten weeks with United, Taylor was selected to tour South America for England, scoring in his first international debut against Chile. Despite fierce competition, Taylor won a regular place on the team and in his last England game scored both goals in the 2-0 victory over France. He went on to score 25 goals in his 33 appearances for United during the 1955-56 campaign culminating in United winning the League.

In 1957, Tommy Taylor scored a hat-trick in the 10-0 victory over Belgian Champions Anderlecht, in United's first ever European Cup game. A year later, Taylor, along with seven other team-mates, was killed at Munich.

BELOW Tommy Taylor, an international striker struck down in his prime

RIGHT Carlos Tevez battles for the ball with Micah Richards of Manchester City

Tevez

LABELLED THE "ARGENTINE prophet for the 21st century" by none other than Diego Maradona himself, Carlos Tevez bears more than a passing resemblance to the player many described as the best in the world during the 1980s. Tevez, born on 5 February 1984 in Buenos Aires, has also tasted success with his national side, winning a gold medal at the 2004 Olympics and starring in the 2006 World Cup.

At club level, Tevez began his professional career with Boca Juniors in 2001 before transferring to Corinthians four years later. After an explosive 2005-06 season that saw him score 25 goals in 38 games, Tevez refused to play for his Brazilian employers and speculation was rife that a move was imminent. West Ham proved to be his destination but concern over the third party who owned his contract led to disputes and an eventual change in Premier League rules.

In his short spell with the club, Tevez helped them win two Premier League titles and a Champions League crown with 34 goals in 98 appearances. Much to the dismay of his adoring fans, he left United to join arch rivals Manchester City in July 2009.

He was sensationally replaced by Michael Owen, the former Liverpool, Real Madrid and Newcastle United forward who most people, apart from Sir Alex Ferguson, thought was past his sell-by date. His goalscoring record though is beyond dispute especially with England where he has scored 40 goals in 89 appearances. If he can perform as well as Larsson – who was bought in a similar fashion a couple of seasons ago – it will be money well spent and could boost Owen's chances of playing for England in the World Cup.

Three Hundred Club

Player	Dates played	Appearances
Ryan Giggs	1991-	805
Bobby Charlton	1956-73	753
Bill Foulkes	1952-70	688
Paul Scholes	1994-	604
Gary Neville	1992-	570
Alex Stepney	1966-78	539
Tony Dunne	1960-73	535
Dennis Irwin	1990-03	529
Joe Spence	1919-33	510
Arthur Albiston	1974-88	485
Roy Keane	1993-05	480
Brian McClair	1987-98	471
George Best	1963-74	470
Mark Hughes	1983-86, 88-95	467
Bryan Robson	1981-94	461
Martin Buchan	1971-83	456
Jack Silcock	1919-34	449
Gary Pallister	1989-98	437
Jack Rowley	1937-55	424
Sammy McIlroy	1971-82	419
Steve Bruce	1987-96	414
Denis Law	1962-73	404
Lou Macari	1972-84	401
Peter Schmeichel	1991-99	398

LEFT Appearances in all competitions to end 2008-09 season

BELOW Ryan Giggs in action during the Premiership match between Chelsea and United at Stamford Bridge in April, 2006

THREE HUNDRED CLUB

BELOW Gary Neville during the Premiership match between Tottenham Hotspur and United at White Hart Lane in April, 2006

Pat Crerand	1962-71	397
Steve Coppell	1975-83	396
Nobby Stiles	1960-71	395
David Beckham	1992-03	394
Allenby Chilton	1939-55	391
Nicky Butt	1992-04	387
Phil Neville	1995-05	386
Mike Duxbury	1980-90	378
Gary Bailey	1978-86	375
Ole Gunnar Solskjaer	1996-07	366
Mikael Silvestre	1999-08	361
Shay Brennan	1957-70	359
Stan Pearson	1937-54	345
Johnny Carey	1937-53	344
John O'Shea	1999-	341
Billy Meredith	1906-21	335
David Sadler	1963-74	335
Charlie Moore	1919-30	328
Alfred Steward	1920-32	326
Clarence Hilditch	1919-32	322
George Wall	1905-15	319
Wes Brown	1996-	317
Fred Erentz	1892-02	310
Alex Bell	1902-13	309
Charlie Roberts	1904-13	302
Ray Bennion	1927-32	301

Treble

THE 1998-99 SEASON PROVED TO be a momentous one for Manchester United with the club becoming the first to add the UEFA Champions League title (formerly the European Cup) to the domestic Double of Premier League and FA Cup.

The FA Cup run will forever be remembered for Ryan Giggs's solo goal which gave United victory over Arsenal in the semi-final replay. Hailed as the greatest-ever FA Cup goal, United were down to ten men following Roy Keane's dismissal when Giggs started his run in his own half and dribbled past five defenders before hammering the ball home. The Premiership title was wrapped up with a 2-1 victory at home to Spurs the week before the FA Cup Final. United's opponents at Wembley were Newcastle United, but goals from substitute and man of the match Teddy Sheringham and Paul Scholes sealed the Double.

In Barcelona four days later, United were trailing Bayern Munich to a Basler free-kick for most of the match. In injury time, Schmeichel came up for a corner and in the confusion Sheringham steered Giggs's mis-hit shot into the net for the equaliser. As the watching millions braced themselves for extra-time, United again won a corner. Ole Gunnar Solskjaer was the player to hit the back of the net this time and spark jubilant celebrations.

ABOVE Alex Ferguson is held aloft by his team as they celebrate victory in the Champions League Final against Bayern Munich at the Nou Camp Stadium in Barcelona, 1999

UEFA Cup

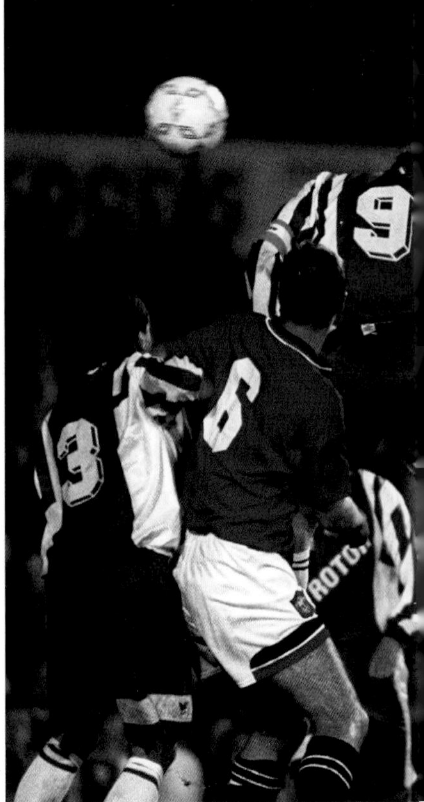

MIDDLE Goalkeeper Peter Schmeichel heads in a goal during the UEFA Cup first round second leg match against Rotor Volgograd at Old Trafford, September 1995

FAR RIGHT Lee Sharpe in action against Rotor Volgograd

UNITED HAVE NEVER REACHED the Final of the UEFA Cup and they have suffered first-round exits on four occasions. Widzew Lodz went through on the away goals rule following a 1-1 draw at Old Trafford in 1980-81 while United lost 2-1 on aggregate against Valencia two years later. The opponents in 1992-93 were Torpedo Moscow and after two goalless games the Russians emerged victorious from the penalty shoot-out.

Rotor Volgograd were the visitors to Old Trafford in September 1995 and it took a headed Peter Schmeichel goal in the dying minutes to preserve United's unbeaten home record in Europe. The 2-2 draw was not enough to see United progress, however, with Rotor claiming a second-round berth on the away goals rule. United did make it to the second round in 1976-77, losing 3-1 on aggregate to Juventus.

The 1984-85 season would take them closest to the trophy when they saw off the challenges of Raba Vasas, PSV Eindhoven and Dundee United on their way to a quarter-final meeting with Videoton. United won the home

leg 1-0 but could not make a breakthrough in the second leg, conceding an equaliser in the first half. Extra-time could not separate the sides and missed penalties by Frank Stapleton and Mark Hughes cost United a place in the semi-final.

Upsets

RIGHT Eric Djemba-Djemba battles Steve Flack of Exeter City during the FA Cup third round match, 2005

UNITED HAVE NOT BEEN THE victims of that many giantkillings in their time and it is the Cup competitions that provide the minnows with opportunity to ruffle a few feathers. In their first ever League Cup campaign in 1960, Third Division Bradford City ousted them from the competition with a 2-1 victory.

There were not many who would have predicted that Second Division York City would take a 3-0 first leg advantage away from Old Trafford and hang on to win 4-3 on aggregate in the 1995-96 League Cup second round. FA Cup upsets have come at the hands of Third Division Bristol Rovers (4-0 third round winners in 1955-56), Second Division Southampton (1-0 winners in the 1975-76 Final) and Third Division Bournemouth (2-0 third round winners in 1983-84).

Many also consider Exeter City's 0-0 draw with United in the third round of the 2004-05 FA Cup to be an upset. Fergie's team of youngsters could not break down the Conference side at Old Trafford, despite the introduction of Ronaldo, Scholes and Alan Smith from the subs bench. United went on to win the replay 2-0 at St James' Park. A draw against Conference side Burton Albion at the same stage in January 2006 was, however, followed by an emphatic 5-0 win at Old Trafford.

Van der Sar

SINCE THE DEPARTURE OF PETER Schmeichel in 1999, the goalposts at Old Trafford have seen nine different goalkeepers at a cost of £20 million. Of the most recent incumbents, Roy Carroll moved to West Ham in the summer of 2005, while Tim Howard did not prove reliable enough to be first choice.

Fabien Barthez was the most successful keeper for the longest time after Schmeichel's departure to Sporting Lisbon, but he was prone to high profile errors. Sir Alex Ferguson signed Edwin Van der Sar in June 2005 in a bid to solve what might have become a goalkeeping crisis. The move worked however, as Van der Sar shored up the back line and helped United to a hat-trick of Premier League titles as well as denying Anelka in the penalty shoot-out to win the Champions League Final.

Having played for Ajax and Juventus and having made more than 150 appearances for Fulham, Van der Sar was in his mid thirties when he signed for the club but old father time had dulled neither his ambition nor his influence.

Age has not been a problem, far from it. In the 2008-09 season, he played 1,311 minutes in the League without conceding a goal. This remarkable feat set a new standard for English, British and European football.

ABOVE Kevin Campbell of West Bromwich Albion is halted by Edwin Van Der Sar

Van Nistelrooy

RIGHT Ruud scores the opening goal from the penalty spot during the Premiership match against Fulham in 2003

BORN 1 JULY 1976, RUUD VAN Nistelrooy's debut for United in August 2001 nearly did not take place after the striker found himself fighting to regain fitness after a knee injury threatened to rob him of his career. He was due to move from PSV Eindhoven and sign for United at the end of the 1999-2000 season, but the problem with his knee meant he had to return to Holland and undergo an extensive rehabilitation process. Once he had recovered he signed for the club for a transfer fee of £19 million and proved to Alex Ferguson and the rest of the team that he had been well worth the wait.

Teddy Sheringham and Andy Cole soon left and Van Nistelrooy became the exceptional striker that United were looking for. During the 2001-02 season he scored 36 goals and went on to set a new Premiership record by scoring in eight consecutive League games which included his first hat-trick for his team when they beat Southampton 6-1. His attitude was even more determined in his second season, scoring 44 goals with 15 of them coming in the last ten matches. But while the European Cup, the FA Cup and the League Cup eluded United, Van Nistelrooy's shooting ability ensured the club brought the Premiership trophy back to Old Trafford.

The start of the 2003-04 season saw him continuing his magnificent form and his goals in ten successive games beat the record of eight set by Liam Whelan in the 1950s. Van Nistelrooy helped United win the FA Cup in 2003-04 with two goals against Millwall in the Final. He had a contract with United that could have lasted at least until June 2008 but he was on his way to Real Madrid in the summer of 2006 after he fell out with Sir Alex.

ABOVE Sir Alex welcomes new signing Ruud van Nistelrooy to Old Trafford in April 2001

Vidic

BELOW Nemanja Vidic controls the ball

THERE AREN'T MANY PLAYERS who win half a dozen trophies in their first three seasons at a new club but that is exactly what Nemanja Vidic has achieved with three Premier League titles, Champions League and Fifa World Club Finals as well as a Carling Cup in 2009.

Born in Yugoslavia on 21 October 1981, Vidic made his professional debut for Red Star Belgrade in 2000 and helped them to the League and Cup double in 2004 before heading for Moscow. Rated as one of the best defenders in Europe, Vidic is also a danger at set pieces and had scored 12 goals in 152 games by the end of the 2008-09 season. With such performances not going unnoticed around the world, United fans were overjoyed to hear that he signed a contract extension in 2007 that keeps the player who has won 40 caps for his native Serbia, at the club until 2012.

Violett

A LOCAL LAD BORN 20 SEPTEMBER 1933, Dennis Viollet was an outstanding striker, particularly during the 1959-60 season when he scored 32 League goals. He signed for United in 1952, having joined Matt Busby's youth scheme after leaving school. He had a tremendous strength despite his slight frame that won him his first-team debut aged 19 alongside Tommy Taylor at Newcastle.

Like Taylor, Viollet won League Championship medals in 1956 and 1957. Renowned for his lightning runs, quick reflexes and intelligent positioning it was surprising he only won two caps for England, against Hungary and Luxembourg in 1960. Despite surviving the Munich air crash, he suffered head injuries which rendered him unable to play until the end of the 1957-58 season when he played as a warm up to the FA Cup Final against Bolton Wanderers. His form suffered for a time but was regained during the following season when his goals helped United finish second in the First Division.

He made 291 appearances in League and Cup competitions scoring a total of 178 goals. He was forced to make way for Denis Law in 1962 and was transferred to Stoke City for £25,000. In more than 200 games he scored 66 goals before leaving in 1967 to play in the North American Soccer League for Baltimore Bays.

Viollet returned home after 18 months and continued to play football in Northern Ireland and for non-League Witton Albion. He coached at Preston and Crewe before returning to America. He returned to Munich in 1997 along with other survivors as a guest of UEFA to attend the European Cup Final.

RIGHT Local lad Dennis Viollet, a Munich survivor who served United well

Whelan

BELOW William 'Liam' Whelan, an Irish prodigy who perished at Munich

BERT WHALLEY SPOTTED WILLIAM Whelan (born 1 April 1935) in 1953 playing with Home Farm FC, the famous Dublin nursery. Liam showed tremendous ball control and would leave opposition defenders stunned with sudden shots. His first match for United was in the 1953 FA Youth Cup Final which they won against Wolves, but he did not enjoy his first-team debut until March 1955.

Matt Busby was anxious about Whelan's lack of confidence. He was a modest player and unsure of his talents, but he won Championship medals in 1956 and 1957 and four caps for Ireland. He was United's leading League scorer in 1956-57 with 26 goals in 39 matches. Despite losing his position as inside-forward to Bobby Charlton, Whelan had travelled to Belgrade with the team in February 1958 and was killed at Munich.

Whiteside

NORMAN WHITESIDE IS ANOTHER Belfast lad to have made it to United. Born 7 May 1965, by the age of ten he had scored more than 100 goals in one season for his school. He went on to be the youngest player, aged 17, to score for United in a match against Stoke City. Sammy McIlroy declared he was "…a man well before his time. We used to joke that he was nine before he was born."

Whiteside was discovered by the same scout as George Best, Bob Bishop, who brought him to Old Trafford as a 13-year-old schoolboy in 1978. He signed professionally for the club in 1981, making his debut, aged just 16, in 1982 as a substitute for United at Brighton. By the age of 20, he had appeared in the World Cup Finals and was on the winning side of FA Cup victories on two occasions. His greatest moment came in the 1985 FA Cup Final when, deep into extra time, he charged down the pitch at Wembley and scored a stunning goal, from what many believed was an impossible angle, to win the Cup for United.

ABOVE Norman Whiteside on the ball for United, 1985

He was an extremely competitive footballer with a fiery temper, culminating in several suspensions and the press nickname of 'Nasty Norman'. Despite playing again in the 1986 World Cup Finals, Whiteside's form was suffering and he struggled with his fitness. He was sold to Everton in 1989 for £75,000, but a knee injury after two years forced early retirement at the age of 26. He left football in 1992 to pursue a career as a podiatrist.

ABOVE Dwight Yorke tussles with Amaral during the Vasco da Gama match in the World Club Championship, 2000

RIGHT Ruud van Nistelrooy celebrates scoring in the penalty shoot-out during the FA Cup Final against Arsenal, May 2005

World Club Championship

UNITED CAUSED A PUBLIC OUT-cry by refusing to defend the FA Cup when they withdrew from the 1999-2000 competition (with the approval of the FA) to compete in the World Club Championship in Rio de Janeiro. The argument was put forward that they entered under pressure from the government, who saw it as supporting England's bid to host the 2006 World Cup. Three games in six days in the searing heat did not improve United's chances of claiming the trophy.

A Dwight Yorke goal earned a draw against Rayos del Necaxa while Nicky Butt scored the consolation goal as United went down 3-1 to Vasco de Gama. Two Quinton Fortune goals in the final group match against South Melbourne meant that although they didn't qualify for the next phase, they did end the trip with a victory.

X-Tra Time

OVER THE YEARS, MANCHESTER United have been involved in drawn Cup matches that have required replays to decide a winner but extra-time can provide a much more exciting finale. In 1887, however, Newton Heath were scratched from the FA Cup following their refusal to play extra-time after a 2-2 draw with Fleetwood Rangers.

When there is no possibility of a replay (becoming more and more common with the modern congested fixture list) and extra-time has been unable to provide a clear winner, the match has to be decided by a penalty shoot-out. United suffered in this manner for the first time in the FA Cup when they lost a second-round replay to Southampton in 1992-93. The 2004-05 FA Cup Final was also memorably decided in this fashion after United had dominated arch-rivals Arsenal during the game but had been unable to find the decisive strike.

Although not technically extra-time, injury time can play a major factor in the result as well. This is easily demonstrated in United's home Premiership clash with Sheffield Wednesday in April 1993. Trailing to a 64th-minute John Sheridan penalty, Steve Bruce popped up in the penalty area to head home the equaliser with four minutes left. It was Bruce who was again on target, heading in the winner six minutes and 12 seconds into injury time.

Youth Team

IT WAS MATT BUSBY WHO PIONEERED the successful tradition of spotting talent in schoolboys and nurturing them. With the introduction of the FA Youth Cup in 1953 came United's domination of the early years of the competition as the Busby Babes went on to win it five times in succession.

RIGHT A youthful David Beckham in action for United Youths

BELOW George Best, another home-grown superstar

Following their initial win, the team – including future stars Bobby Charlton and Duncan Edwards – was invited to attend the 1953-54 Blue Stars International Youth Tournament in Zurich. The next crop of youngsters to claim the title included George Best, David Sadler and John Aston Junior in 1963-64 and it would be another 18 years before a United youth team again graced the Final. Following Alex Ferguson's restructuring of the Old Trafford youth system, the trophy was brought back to Old Trafford in 1992, this time with a side including Nicky Butt, the Neville brothers, Paul Scholes, David Beckham and Ryan Giggs.

Two more wins followed in 1994-95 and 2002-03 to leave United standing on top of the pile with nine titles although a tenth crown proved to be, hopefully temporarily, beyond them as they lost 4-3 on penalties to Liverpool in 2007 after the game had been tied at 2-2 after extra time. Amazingly, 6,492 spectators attended the 'junior Manchester derby' in February 2006 that saw City knock United out of the Youth Cup by a single goal.

Zero

MANCHESTER UNITED KEPT A total of 1,619 clean sheets in their 5,044 matches to the end of the 2007-08 season. Of these, 1,301 came in League matches with a further 149 in the FA Cup, 54 in the League Cup and 104 in Europe. United saw their Premiership record for the most clean sheets in a campaign (24 achieved in 1994-95 when they ironically finished second behind Blackburn Rovers) broken by Chelsea during the 2004-05 season when they only conceded a miserly 15 goals. Peter Schmeichel's 694 minutes without conceding a goal has also since been extended to 1,024 by Peter Cech. Peter Schmeichel's 694 minutes without conceding a goal has since been extended to 1,311 by Edwin Van der Sar – between Nasri's strike for Arsenal on 8 November 2008 and Peter Lovenkrands' opener for Newcastle on 4 March 2009.

ABOVE Peter Schmeichel celebrates in May 1999

Other books also available:

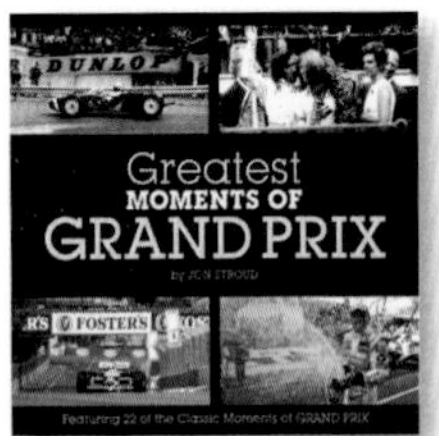

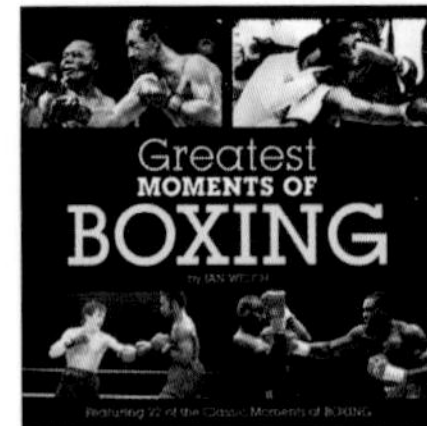

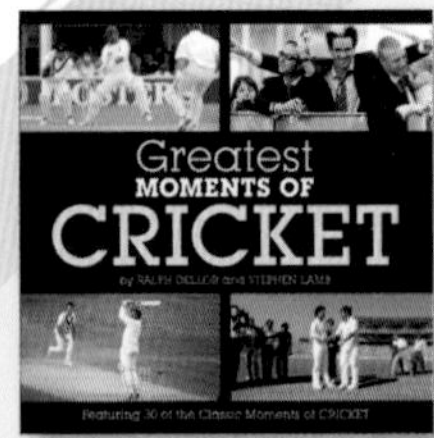

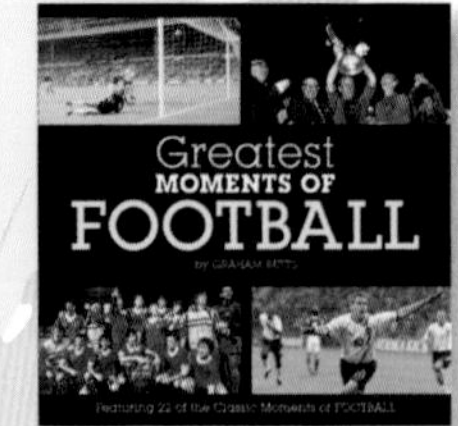

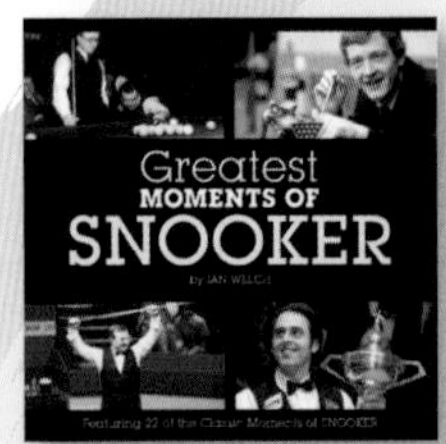

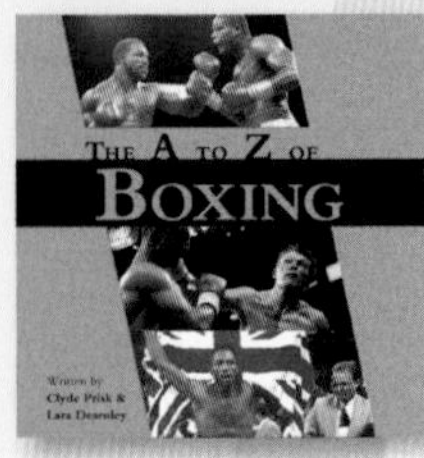

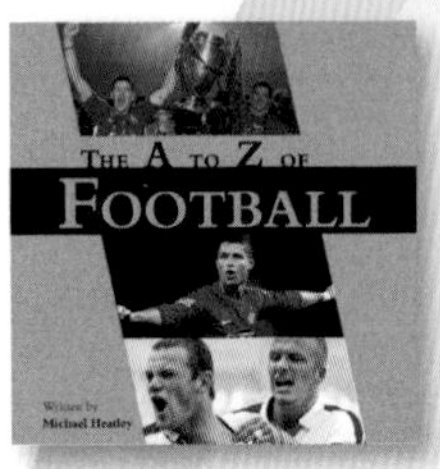

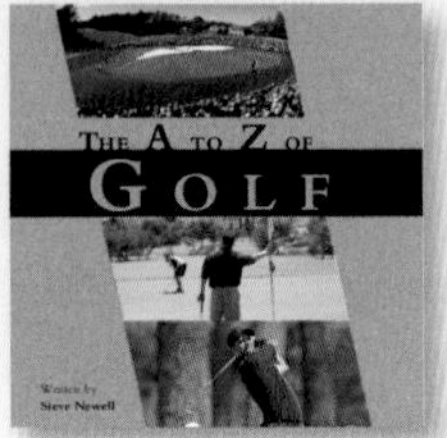

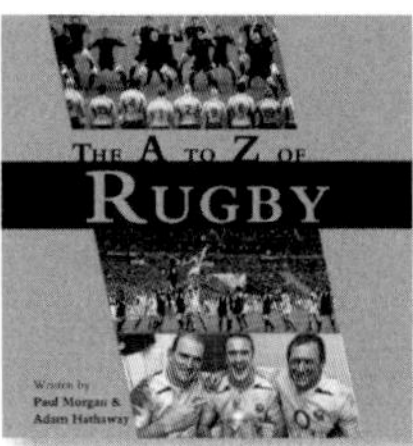

Available from all major stockists